School Public Relations

THE LIBRARY OF EDUCATION

A Project of The Center for Applied Research in Education, Inc.

G. R. Gottschalk, Director

Categories of Coverage

I	II	III
Curriculum and Teaching	Administration, Organization, and Finance	Psychology for Educators

IV	V	VI
History, Philosophy, and Social Foundations	Professional Skills	Educational Institutions

School Public Relations

JAMES J. JONES

Chairman,
Department of Educational Administration
Temple University

The Center for Applied Research in Education, Inc.
New York

Foreword

Because public schools are owned and operated by the people of the state and of the local community, there is an obligation on the part of boards of education, administrative officers, and other school employees to take the public into their confidence and to provide them with the information they need in order that they understand the total educational program. The public must be made aware of the opportunities that are available for their participation in the total social task of making good schools even better.

Experience has demonstrated conclusively that the more thoroughly citizens understand their schools and the more they become involved in school improvement, less is the effort required for obtaining public moral and financial support which is necessary if educational progress is to be made.

In the light of this experience more and more school systems are consciously trying to open channels of communication with citizens in order to make their voice heard. Some are succeeding remarkably well while others are finding it difficult to achieve this objective. The difference generally lies in how much insight and understanding the school's professional personnel possess in regard to principles and procedures of public relations.

This volume aims to help school officials and other school workers become acquainted with the fundamental concepts underlying the development (or improvement) of a public relations program. It discusses the characteristics of an efficient program—how it should be conducted; what materials are needed; what the responsibilities of the employees are (ranging from the members of the board of education to the custodial staff); how to interpret the role of the school plant; and what techniques to use to appraise outcomes. It is not a book of answers, rather, it is one suggesting how personnel can find their own answers to *local* educational needs and problems. The book's unique feature is that it combines in one small volume the

▼

principles and procedures involved in planning and implementing a sound public relations program.

School Public Relations will no doubt step up an already growing awareness of the need for public relations. It will help direct public school efforts toward communicating with parents and other involved citizens. Only with their support and constructive interest can public education continue to improve and move forward.

LESLIE W. KINDRED
Professor of Educational Administration
Temple University

School Public Relations

James J. Jones

With the present-day interest in public education, the matter of good school public relations is of paramount importance to superintendents, boards of education, and teachers. Dr. James J. Jones has written competently on the topic and his book is a useful guide to all those engaged in public education. If the information and advice given in this book were understood and applied, the public climate for education would be improved considerably.

Dr. Jones carefully delineates the nature and purpose of school relations. He devoted one chapter to showing the interrelationships that exist between the school and the community, pointing out that knowledge of the community and knowledge of the school must be exchanged for better understanding between the two. Methods of organization and administration of public relations are presented in such a way as to demonstrate how this organization fits into the educational system.

Another very useful chapter points out the responsibilities of each of the major roles in the schools—the relation of teachers, administrators, and non-professional personnel to public relations, all are presented in an operational manner. In the remaining chapters, the author discusses various techniques and media that can be used to promote public relations; the relation of the school plant to public relations; and ways of evaluating the worth of a program.

Dr. Jones is Professor of Education at Temple University. He has written widely on school public relations and has been a consultant in that field. The information available in this book should be an aid to anyone interested in improving the image of the schools in America.

DANIEL E. GRIFFITHS
Content Editor

Contents

ix

School Public Relations

CHAPTER I

The Nature and Purpose of School Public Relations

Only in recent years has much interest been evidenced in studying the problems and issues of school public relations—that is, the relations between the public and their public schools. A close look at the literature on education before the middle 1920s reveals little of value in the realm of research and ideas concerning public relations.

The Meaning of Public Relations

A large number of authorities have defined "public relations" with some degree of agreement. Carter Good,[1] editor of *The Dictionary of Education,* states that "public relations" is the formal activity of improving the relations of a school within a community. It is an activity concerned with giving information to the public about the school or with creating good will for the school.

Harry L. Stearns[2] says "public relations is the opening of two-way channels of communications between the citizens of a community, who possess and support the schools, and the professional people who conduct them." This definition implies room for mutual interaction along the two-way street.

A similar meaning is given by Reeder,[3] who states that public relations is the phase of educational administration that seeks to bring a harmonious working relationship between the schools and the public which the schools serve. This meaning embodies a working relationship that secures effective results.

In the present volume "public relations" is defined in a broad

---

[1] Carter V. Good, ed., *Dictionary of Education* (New York: McGraw-Hill Book Co., 1959), p. 430.

[2] Harry L. Stearns, *Community Relations and the Public Schools* (Englewood Cliffs, N.J.: Prentice-Hall, Inc., 1955), p. 7.

[3] Ward G. Reeder, *An Introduction to Public School Relations* (New York: The Macmillan Co., 1953), p. 1.

1

sense and designates all the functions and relationships that pertain in a two-way exchange of ideas between school and community and that establish the basis for joint understanding. "Public relations" and "school public relations" will be used interchangeably with "school-community relations." To separate public relations from other aspects of school administration is almost impossible, as every part of the work of the schools has some bearing upon the relationship of the schools and the community.

The Need for Public Relations

Public relations affects all phases of the educational program. Consequently, persons who work with the program and with children see a need for a better understanding of the program and all of its detail. Currently one may find many people working with the public schools—such as administrators, supervisors, teachers, board members, graduate students, professors of education, and others—who are actively involved in studying or administering school public relations.

The ever-increasing emphasis now being placed upon school public relations as a vital phase in the total process of the education of the child is revealed through a comprehensive reading of the literature in the field of public school administration. The large amount of space devoted to public relations in professional books and journals gives further evidence of the general recognition of the importance of establishing proper interpretative relations between school and community.

While there has been a vast increase in the volume of research in school public relations, relatively few problems in the field have been completely or adequately solved. Many persons doing research in school administration have pointed to several reasons why administrators should be concerned with public relations. A review of some of these reasons follows.

Changing school patterns. During earlier periods of American education it was relatively easy for pupils, parents, and the public to know and to understand what was happening at school and in the community. But changes in regard to purpose, content, and teaching methods, along with the increasing size and costs of schools, have tended to confuse the general public and to leave them without adequate information. Today's complex and urbanized society demands that public school pupils be provided educational experiences quite different from many of those which present-day parents themselves received when they were in school.

Citizen information. The limited and often inaccurate information possessed by citizens concerning the work of the schools further points up the need for more adequate public relations. A classic study on citizen knowledge by William H. Todd[4] analyzed the responses of 7,000 parents in seventeen cities to a long series of true-false questions concerning the board of education, the curriculum, finance, buildings, pupils, the teacher, the superintendent, school organization, and administration. He found that citizens know about half of what they should, or even must, know about their schools if they are to give reasonably intelligent consideration to public school affairs. Further, he discovered that citizens have little idea as to the number of children their community must educate, what the community is spending on education, the number of teachers required, or the minimum wage paid teachers in any department. In the years since this early study there has not been anything to refute these findings.

Possibilities for improvement. In many instances people do not understand or conceive what is possible in good schools. As schools developed new aims in regard to educating youth, they have not always expressed them in a manner that is easily understood, and have thereby provided a source of confusion to the layman. A tendency to look with suspicion upon contemplated school changes characterizes the attitude of far too many communities. As a consequence, one may find a public tendency to conserve the "status quo" and to oppose both professionals and nonprofessionals who try to lead the way toward improvement. Many educators accept the fact that the performance of the majority of schools in the country is far below what it might be if all that is known about the science or art of education were put into practice.

Changing faculty status. For many years our public schools were staffed and taught by people who relieved themselves from other jobs long enough to give some time to the training of youth, although their principal preparation and interest were not in the field

---

[4] William H. Todd, *What Citizens Know About Their Schools* (New York: Columbia University, Contributions to Education, 1927).

of education. Today, education has developed and improved as a profession and both interest and preparation have to meet higher standards than before. Changes in both administrative organization and teaching methodology have been revised in light of recent research and experimentation. These developments need to be understood by the public.

Public opinion of teachers. Neither the reluctance of the public to accord teachers freedom in the classroom nor the lack of appreciation of the role of the teacher in community affairs is in keeping with the improved professional training required of teachers. The public may think the work of the teacher is significant, but not as significant as that of people in other professions. Teachers seem to occupy a secondary position in the eyes of the community despite the fact that many of them have undergone longer periods of study and preparation than people in some other professions. Teachers should participate in community affairs to the same extent that members of other professions do. They should not be expected to spend as much free time in community work as they devote to teaching. Teachers want to be free to experiment in the classroom and to live a normal life in the community.

Pressure groups. Another need for public relations is indicated by the increasing number of board policies and state statutes which have been passed as indirect results of some pressure groups. Much of this legislation and many other policies restrict the educational program and limit what the teacher is able to do. The real need is for the administrator to be able to identify and to analyze pressure groups and to discover their purposes and actions. Only then can better relations be established.

Increased Scope of Public Relations

It has become increasingly clear in recent years that it is impossible for the educator to have a relatively free hand in developing an enriched educational program if the public is left behind in its understanding of education. It is believed that a community with its vision of the possibilities of education made clear through study and discussion of what good schools are doing elsewhere can stimulate teachers to provide constantly richer educational experiences for children.

Educators have now come to realize that the schools need more good will from the public than ever before. A particular need exists for the type of good will that results from an intelligent understanding by citizens of the aims, the scope, the achievements, and the problems of the school system. There is a growing opinion among educators that ineffective public relations policies are proving very costly to schools, and this conviction is causing a determined effort to meet real issues in the social interpretation of the school.

Beginning of public relations. In a sense, public relations in connection with public schools began with the first school. No public school ever operated in a social vacuum apart from the society it served. In every school and community thousands of opportunities arise for affecting public relations in some degree. Even the most casual contacts tend to influence the public toward the school, either favorably or unfavorably. Every school activity and every contact between members of the school personnel and the children and adults of the community has great potentialities for public relations.

It may be said that public relations in the American schools had its beginning in 1837 when the first state board of education was created in Massachusetts through the efforts of James G. Carter and Horace Mann.[5] Horace Mann, the first secretary of the board, began a most remarkable work of molding public opinion, and soon became the leader of school organizations in the United States. Each year Horace Mann organized campaigns to explain to the people the meaning and importance of education. He was so successful that he started a great common school revival which led to the regeneration of schools throughout the northeastern states. Perhaps no one did more than he to establish in the minds of the American people the conception that education should be universal, nonsectarian, and free.

Formal recognition. Public relations has only recently developed as a subject deemed worthy of study in education. If the attention public relations has received since the early twenties may be taken as a criterion, the subject is rapidly coming to be recognized as one of major importance. Every new function accepted by the school carries with it the need for understanding and cooperation between school and community forces. Public school relations assume increasing importance as a process in the administrator's

---

[5] Ellwood P. Cubberley, *The History of Education* (New York: Houghton-Mifflin Co., 1920), p. 689.

agendum in direct proportion to the widening scope of his other educational activities.

Public relations problems have always existed in public school administration, just as they have in every large business organization. However, not until recent years has there been any formal recognition of the function and value of public relations in our public schools. Business has realized the value of sound public policies to a much larger degree than has the public schools. Since the schools belong to the people, and since the people establish and maintain them, it is essential that the people know what the program of education is in their institutions. As administration has become more scientific, the public relations program has come to play a most essential part in the functioning of a system-wide—as well as an individual—school program.

Increased interest of the public. The increasingly close relationship between the school and the community has been one of the most pressing developments in contemporary American education. Because the school's success is dependent upon this relationship, the school should try to make it as close and cordial as possible.

If the people are taken into the confidence of the school officials and helped to share information concerning the purposes, conditions, and the needs of the schools, they are more likely to give continuous support to the schools. On the other hand, if they are kept ignorant of these matters, they are likely to be skeptical of such things as tax increases, building programs, bond issues, and curricular changes.

Throughout the nation at the present time there is an upsurge of public interest in the schools. Seldom has such an interest been shown and never before have the schools been in greater need of public understanding and support. Teamwork can accomplish much if educational leadership will recognize and grasp the opportunities now at hand.

The aim of public relations in our schools has been to keep the public informed concerning the purposes, accomplishments, conditions, and needs of the schools. When the public has been informed it is believed that the average citizen will be better qualified and more inclined to cooperate with the schools. Like other phases of effective school administration, public relations has been designed to advance the welfare of the individuals for whom the schools exist—namely, the pupils.

Lay participation. The participation of lay people in school planning has public relations significance. It formally acknowledges a fact too often overlooked by school personnel—that is, that the total educative process is not able to avoid the use of agencies and individuals other than those in the school. The home remains one of the most important educational forces, especially with regard to such matters as attitudes and values. Citizen participation in educational matters can aid the school indirectly and have a profound influence upon the home. Lay participation can effectively serve as an essential means of parent education.

The citizens have a worthy contribution to make to the school, for if the educational effort is to achieve expressive success, a degree of coordination and planning regarding the educational experiences of the child must exist. Very little may be accomplished in the reading tastes of the child if the school and the home are each unaware of what the other is doing, or if they are operating at cross-purposes. Significantly, the conclusion is thus reached that what is the best educational practice is the best public relations—or, good public relations involving much participation is sound education and in the interest of both children and adults.

Significance of Public Relations

In early American history, schools were the outgrowth of the recognition of the community of the vital need for education. The school was considered by the community to be an integral part of its organization. Schools were publicly originated, controlled, and supervised. Public relations programs were unnecessary because of the position of the school as a center of the community; for the same reason, teachers participated in community affairs to a considerable degree. There was no hard and fast division between the administrative and supervisory processes, nor in the earlier years was either process considered a professional function. There was little need for an organized program of public relations during a time when lay interest and control were so active.

The American public school embraces the principles of democracy in rather general terms. In order to fulfill the goals of the American way of life a large investment in public education has become necessary. The vertical structure of the public schools includes kindergarten and elementary grades, junior and senior high school grades, and, in selected communities, the junior college. Thus the public has made an initial investment and has added to it large annual sums for the continued support of public education.

The extent of this investment is directly related to community attitudes toward public education and the ability of the community to support it. Since public schools belong to the people, who have established and supported them in accordance with economic conditions and social attitudes, it behooves the public school officials to work for better community understanding. It is important that the public comprehend the type and quality of education their money buys and how it contributes to our democratic way of life.

Public relations seeks the support of the people for the maintenance and the direction of an institution which is basic to popular government as we know it today. The schools are expected to make a significant contribution to the future as children who are being educated in our schools today become the adults of tomorrow. The type of job that is needed makes public relations a necessity, for education can grow and expand only as the public becomes conscious of the role that schools play in our society.

Purposes of Public Relations

In any effective public relations program it is imperative that those persons who are responsible for its origin, maturation, and growth comprehend the goals such a program attempts to achieve. To a large extent, the purposes of a public relations program are conditioned by what the school people believe about education and the ways in which public relations may become an agent of the school and community. Purposes of public relations have been treated by many authorities, and their collective opinions are listed below:

1. To explain to the community the school system's philosophy of education, its aims, and its means of achieving these aims.
2. To interpret the educational program to the people of the com-

munity in a way that will encourage them to take pride in and support their schools.

3. To establish confidence in the on-going institution.

4. To indicate to the public that they are receiving full value for moneys expended on education.

5. To develop an understanding of what is possible in education when adequate support is provided.

6. To acquaint the public with the trends in education.

7. To correct misunderstandings or errors.

8. To help the public feel some sense of responsibility for the quality of education the school distributes.

School public relations has become a much broader concept than mere publicity or interpretation. It involves human relations or the way in which one relates himself to his surroundings. Since many publics, rather than one general opinion, must be satisfied, the school must always keep the child's welfare as its focus, along with the essential needs of society. The Twenty-Eighth Yearbook of the American Association of School Administrators[6] gives the following purposes of public relations:

1. To inform the public as to the work of the school.

2. To establish confidence in schools.

3. To rally support for proper maintenance of the educational program.

4. To develop awareness of the importance of education in a democracy.

5. To improve the partnership concept by uniting parents and teachers in meeting the educational needs of the children.

6. To integrate the home, school, and community in improving the educational opportunities for all children.

7. To evaluate the offering of the school in meeting the needs of the children of the community.

8. To correct misunderstandings as to the aims and activities of the school.

General Scope of Treatment

The organization of this book gives some indication of the steps involved in planning a public relations program. Chapter I identifies the nature and purpose of public relations. It gives insights into the

---

[6] The American Association of School Administrators, *Public Relations for America's Schools* (Washington, D.C.: The Association, Twenty-Eighth Yearbook, 1952), p. 14.

needs and scope of public relations and provides an overview to the remaining chapters. Chapter II identifies the information that is needed to understand and work with the community. It includes ways and means of securing data about the community and its citizens, as well as about the structural and functional aspects of the community and their affect upon the understanding of the schools.

Chapter III treats the organization and administration of public relations. It reviews existing types of organization and the responsibilities of the school board and the superintendent in developing and administering such a program. Other factors that influence organization are reviewed.

Chapter IV reviews the staff and their relationships to public relations. It treats the various responsibilities of the members of the staff.

Techniques of public relations involving information for the public and channels of communication are presented in Chapter V. The school plant is treated in Chapter VI.

Chapter VII describes methods of evaluating public relations programs and their effects. Chapter VIII provides a brief summary of the book.

CHAPTER II

Understanding and
Working with the Community

Understanding the Community

Understanding the community is a factor to be reckoned with in developing any plan of action for public relations. In many instances the community is as deeply concerned with what happens in schools as are school people themselves. To each parent with a child in school what happens in the school is of paramount importance.[1] It appears to be difficult, if not impossible, to argue against the proposition that formal education is necessarily and unavoidably concerned with social change. It is rather interesting to note that nowhere in the literature does one find support for the proposition that formal education should attempt to perpetuate precisely that societal condition which existed at the particular time of writing.[2] There is always some suggestion that the social situation ought to be, to some degree, different. One example of such treatment is Grace Graham's *The Public School in the American Community*,[3] which has as its major purpose the interpretation of the school's role in American society. Primarily a text in educational sociology, it represents the application to education of some knowledge from the social sciences which aids in understanding the school as a social institution. Yet no one volume can include all the evidence that might be cited on any issue.

In attempting to understand the community through the help of sociology, the administrator ought to be guided by the warning given

---

[1] *See* Jean D. Grambs, *Education in a Transition Community* (Miami, Fla.: The National Conference of Christians & Jews, Inc., 1958), p. 68.

[2] Milosh Muntyan, "Community," in *Encyclopedia of Educational Research* (New York: The Macmillan Co., 1960), p. 312.

[3] Grace Graham, *The Public School in the American Community* (New York: Harper & Row, Publishers, 1963).

by Gross.[4] It is his contention that the sociologist restricts the variables he deals with while the administrator must deal with multidimensional forces containing many elements that are unique to the school situation. The administrator cannot afford to overlook any factor that may have a bearing on the specific problem with which he is concerned. Often the administrative task is to isolate and to weigh the critical variables that are at play in his particular and unique situation and then to make decisions based on these calculations. He ought to see the situation in its entirety. The school administrator who uses sociological findings in his work must exercise caution when making direct application of them to public schools.

There are many variables to be found in every community, and the evidence indicates that the community leadership role of the administrator is constantly increasing. As a result, he needs to know more and more about the community and its relationship to education.

The following paragraphs provide four sources of data which school administrators and school personnel may find helpful in understanding communities. These are: census reports, surveys, opinion studies, and principles of public relations.

The United States Census reports. Certainly the superintendent and a large number of school persons throughout a school system will want to make an effort to take the public into account in planning for effective public relations. In order to understand and work with the community, the school administrator needs certain types of information or facts about the community. An excellent source of data about communities is the United States Bureau of the Census. Most of the facts used by the Bureau are collected once in each decade and published in a bulletin for each state.

An administrator can find many useful data concerning such population characteristics of his community as color by sex, race by sex, age by race and sex, citizenship and nativity of population twenty-one years old and over, and years of schooling completed by persons twenty-five years old and over. In addition, information may be obtained about those twenty-five years of age and over, in regard

---

[4] Neal Gross, "The Use and Abuse of Sociological Inquiry in Training Programs for Educational Administrators," *The Social Sciences and Educational Administration* (Edmonton, Canada: The Department of Educational Administration of The University of Canada and The University Council for Educational Administration, 1963), pp. 27–28.

to marital status by race, married couples, families, households, and the country of birth of the foreign-born population. Data about employment status, labor force, and incomes of families are also provided. Generally, one volume gives information on communities of 2,500 population or less and another gives information on communities with more than 2,500 population.

Surveys. During recent years survey research has become widespread and is now almost the center of market research and opinion polling. It has attracted the attention of those charged with determining educational policy, those involved in its administration, and educational scholars interested in school problems. School administrators operate within a type of setting involving several publics. Included in these publics are pupils, teachers, parents, taxpayers, the general public, and several sectors of this public with varying influence, interest, and involvement in school affairs.[5] With the continued population growth and the increased centralization of schools, these publics have become so large and so significant to school functions that a survey type of research is crucial in helping one keep apprised of conditions.

There is virtually no known limit to the information that can be gathered by survey research procedures. Yet, in spite of its usefulness, a full-scale survey is not something that can be used easily or cheaply. School executives often employ professional surveys conducted by educational service and research bureaus of state and private universities or by similar research groups to gather information about the school and community. Survey reports give to the public school official and the general public an impartial evaluation of the work of the schools. Recommendations which grow out of the survey findings help to form the basis upon which the public relations program may be founded. The survey reveals the nature of the community, its people, its resources, its industries, its institutions, and some of its problems. It may be comprehensive or it may deal with one or more aspects of community life. Phases such as youth, occupations, industry, wealth, recreation, or juvenile delinquency offer opportunity for community study. All available sources of information should be studied carefully and utilized in building the program. More recently, surveys have been conducted with the effective help

---

[5] Stephen B. Withey, "Survey Research Methods," in *Encyclopedia of Educational Research* (New York: The Macmillan Co., 1960), p. 1447.

of local lay personnel. These surveys, called cooperative surveys, have tended to build better school and community understanding.

Harold L. O'Neal's[6] study of cooperative surveys in Indiana analyzed the adequacy of and the changes associated with cooperative school building surveys conducted by the Division of Research and Field Services, School of Education, Indiana University, which have been published as issues of the School Survey Series. Data were secured from a survey of opinion from the school officials in eight school districts where Indiana University school surveys had been conducted. School officials in the eight school districts have accepted and put into use eighty-four of the total 115 recommendations directed toward the improvement of existing conditions in the various school districts. They have indicated that eighteen other recommendations will be used when the time is appropriate. Of the total number of recommendations, only thirteen have not been used. This study illustrates the use of the cooperative survey in improving school plant and school finances through observed changes in operation. Likewise, as one phase of its operation, each separate study carried recommendations for school-community relations, and thus promoted a better understanding of the community.

Casual observation is inadequate as a method of inquiry, especially where many opinions and large sums of money are involved. The opinion of an administrator is frequently formed by the strata of the public with which he associates. Surveys help provide information that is more representative of the total community than of local groups.

Opinion studies. In order to discover the quantity and types of information possessed by citizens, careful attention should be focused upon the techniques of opinion polling. In opinion polling there are four principal problems: selection of an adequate and representative sample, development of the questions to be used, choice of a method of presenting these questions to members of the sample, and interpretation of the data. Certainly the major pitfall in public opinion research lies in the interpretation, not in the method. One must remember that public opinion is largely dynamic and can

---

[6] Harold L. O'Neal, "Adequacy and Changes Associated with Conducting Selected Cooperative School Building Surveys," *Thesis Abstract Series, No. 5, Studies in Education,* School of Education, Indiana University, Bloomington, 1954, pp. 167–72.

change suddenly. An opinion study is valid only for a given issue and a given time. Therefore, administrators should exercise caution in the application of public opinion polling techniques to educational issues. This caution is in no way intended to obviate the use of an excellent source of data for educators.

Studies of public opinion can provide us with information about how the people in the community feel concerning certain issues and what they want from the schools. Once public opinion has been ascertained, the administrator is in a better position to communicate with the community in a meaningful manner. For example, do the people of your school district really want a kindergarten program at public expense? Is a community college high on their list of priorities? Should neighborhood schools be broken up by bussing school pupils to other communities to foster integration? Should new school plants have swimming pools? An administrator would be in position to make better judgments with information from the public on such issues as these.

The importance of opinion studies of the community are well stated by Hedlund in regard to how they affect schools and communities:

> They reveal areas of misinformation and ignorance so that the proper school officials may take measures to correct the situation before some antagonistic group takes advantage of the situation.[7]

Information gathered through opinion studies helps educate the community on issues and problems. Polls of this type give the administrator data not distorted by special interest and pressure groups. If opinion polls are to be useful they must be implemented by good administration and leadership.

Principles of public relations. A principle is a generalized statement through which otherwise unrelated data are systematized and interpreted.[8] Principles are necessary guides to action. The understanding, integration, and application of the principles of public relations into the administrative and staff functions of any school system are a vital and determining factor in the final analysis of the effectiveness of the school system. The basic principles are

---

[7] Paul A. Hedlund, "Measuring Public Opinion on School Issues," *American School Board Journal,* CXVI (April, 1948), p. 29.

[8] Carter V. Good, *Dictionary of Education* (New York: McGraw-Hill Book Co., 1959).

the framework which helps the administrator establish direction in meeting the needs of a sound public relations program. The principles which serve this function for the administrator are the result of studies and the evaluation of existing programs considered to be effective as judged by their educational philosophy, their objectives, and the administrative policies in their most acceptable and practical aspects. No argument is presented here that the principles suggested in this section are infallible.

Many authorities have treated the guiding principles of public relations, and their findings may be helpful in planning public relations programs. A review of the literature in the field of public relations has produced many principles which will be presented here, among which are some that have been used by many people and are in the public domain. Others are more restricted and can be found only by extensive research.

A consensus of principles of public relations by a number of authorities in educational administration is listed below:

1. Public relations should be based upon a clear understanding of the objectives and functions of education.

2. Public relations should recognize the legal responsibility of state and local educational authorities.

3. The public relations program should reach the whole community.

4. There should be well thought-out long and short term objectives.

5. The board of education should adopt a policy based upon the recommendations of the superintendent for a public relations program.

6. The effectiveness of any public school is conditioned by the degree of public confidence the school enjoys.

7. A citizen's interest and wholesome attitude in respect to public education are conditioned by correct information.

8. A sound program of public relations requires high staff morale.

9. The public relations program should cover all aspects of school activities, with proportionate attention given to each according to its relative merit.

10. The financial support for all the various agencies should come from the regular school budget.

John M. Hickey studied the public relations programs of the schools of eighty-three large cities of the United States and found eight principles that were acceptable to more than 50 per cent of the school systems. These are:

1. Needs, aspirations, and shortcomings of the community should be understood in directing the public school relations program.

2. Education is a social process in which the child comes to share more and more in the total community consciousness of which he is a part.

3. Mutual interaction of the objectives of community organizations with those of the schools should result in the greatest good for the children.

4. Social agencies of the community should be understood and used in the school program to meet the needs of the children.

5. Personal aggrandizement should be avoided.

6. There should be thorough agreement as to the desirable aims of community life, of the place and function of the home, the school, and each agency of the community.

7. Commencement programs should be built around the aims of education.

8. Printed material should be able to be understood by a person with a fifth grade level of education.[9]

In communities where schools direct a well planned program of public relations, the rate of change to better educational practices may be greater. The logical and challenging result of a program which increases the understanding of a group of leading citizens will be that the group, knowing better the true possibilities of education, will expect better practices in its school.

It is necessary to point out to the public what improvement has been made in the past and what types of improvement are needed in the future. Many times the public does not understand the needs that are being stated by the professional people. Too frequently the community is poorly prepared to act when an emergency issue is put before it because the educators have failed to provide a means for the people to participate in the process of planning. Guides to action are necessary at all times. Principles of school-community relations may be helpful in the development of an effective public relations program, but their limitations should also be kept in mind. In far too many instances the principles have become highly generalized statements with little meaning. It becomes the job of the administrator and especially of the public relations director to utilize the principles of public relations in a way that promotes better understanding of the community.

---

[9] John M. Hickey, "The Direction of Public Relations in Cities of the United States" (Unpublished doctoral dissertation, University of Pittsburgh, 1945), p. 321.

Citizen Knowledge About Schools

It is reasonable to believe that most of today's parents want to know about their children's schools, from the broad aspects of philosophy and curriculum to some of the instructional detail of classroom procedure. Parents are interested in having their children taught by competent teachers; they are interested in how their children are taught and how they are getting along with other children in school. But having a desire for knowledge about the school and making the effort necessary to secure it are not always compatible. Nor do all parents seek knowledge about their children's schools. The following areas give some indications of how parents think with regard to schools.

Purposes of education.   Community attitudes toward the purpose and function of public education vary widely. Some citizens feel that children should not be educated in the public schools, but that such education should be wholly a parochial or parental concern. Others believe that the public school should restrict itself to an elementary program based upon limited financial support. Still others believe in the traditional academic pattern of elementary and secondary education, with major emphasis upon college preparation and little thought given to vocational work. Other citizens believe in a modern educational program which could be offered only with a strong, well organized, varied, and abundantly financed program.

Since the schools belong to the public, the great responsibility of determining the aims of the American schools rightfully belongs to the citizenry as a whole. Yet much of this area of parental knowledge is marred by inadequate information and indifference.

In a study of printed lay opinions, Doyle M. Bortner[10] analyzed the attitudes and opinions of the general public toward education during a twenty-five year period from 1923 to 1947. He reviewed 274 articles from fifteen selected periodicals. An attempt was made to determine relationships between lay views and socio-economic conditions as well as between lay views and types of readers for whom the publications were intended. Some of his conclusions point up the need for increased citizen knowledge about schools:

---

[10] Doyle M. Bortner, "A Study of Published Lay Opinions on Educational Programs and Problems," *Education*, LXXI (June, 1951), 641–51.

1. Laymen are far more concerned with public than with private schools.

2. Laymen are more concerned about curriculum than about any other specific school problem.

3. Laymen are not agreed in their basic views on fundamental issues; the chief controversy is that of functionalism versus conventionalism.

4. A well balanced picture of lay opinion on educational programs and problems is not likely to result from readings confined to a few magazines.

Laymen need current information in order to understand innovations in school practices, and they need to read more than one point of view.

Values of education. If one judges the values of education by tangible changes taking place in our society and in state education programs, such as improved literacy, increased legal minimum age of compulsory attendance, better preparation standards for public school teachers and administrators, and the constantly increasing investment in school plants and equipment along with improved teaching aids, he can hardly feel that educational values are not thoroughly understood by the general public. The American dream of success is often associated with the public schools, as many families are financially unable to educate their children in private schools. Nevertheless, the values associated with education are attached not to public schools alone, but to private schools as well.

Other values attributed to education include enabling persons to move up the economic and social ladder of opportunity, increased incomes, comfortable livelihoods, and early retirement. Business and industrial leaders are concerned about public education since consumer demands tend to increase when levels of education increase. The United States Chamber of Commerce can provide data to support this contention. Even labor and agriculture have come to think of education as an investment in people. Of course, our American way of life is dependent upon an educated citizenry. Long ago Jefferson expressed the concept that a democracy could work only with an educated citizenry.

A very interesting and detailed study of voters and their attitudes toward schools was made by the Institute for Community Research of Stanford University.[11] The institute attempted to discover those

---

[11] Richard V. Carter, "Voters and Their Schools," *The Phi Delta Kappan,* XLIX (February, 1961), 244–49.

factors which affected voter involvement in school affairs—that is, their school and non-school attitudes and activities, as well as their community behavior. The data for this study were collected through interviews held with 900 registered voters before and after a bond election, 2,524 registered voters in three urban areas (from the southwest, the midwest, and the Pacific coast), 769 staff members in a midwest school district, and, in still another school district, 732 husbands and wives who were registered voters.

According to this study, the parent is still more concerned about his child's successful competition than with the nation's success in competition. This does not mean that he thinks national interests are less important, but he is in a much better position to evaluate his child's success and, by inference, to judge the school's performance.[12] A second discovery of significance is that an accurate picture of voters' values with respect to education is marked by their lack of participation in educational matters. Few voters were involved in determining school policy and half of those interviewed were without values sufficient to compel their attention to school matters.

Three conclusions of this study are significant. These are: (1) education is too important an undertaking for the public to neglect completely; (2) schools need more attention from the voters, and many voters now feel that such attention has no efficacy; and (3) school leaders should consider offering formal instruction on the subject of educational institutions, so that future voters will know as much about schools in general as they know about the schools they attended.[13]

Likewise, it may be said that voters have a responsibility to maintain their faith in the potential of education in general, regardless of their feelings about the product of their school in particular. They have a responsibility to commit themselves to participation regardless of their satisfaction. It is part of their responsibility to help overcome the obstacles which come between themselves and the school. The great need is for productive participation in school affairs.

Need for change.   It is as difficult to measure parental attitude toward education as it is to measure changes in attitude toward

---

[12] *Ibid.,* p. 245.
[13] *Ibid.,* pp. 248–49.

education. First, the parents ought to be assisted in understanding that numerous changes in the school and community are taking place. Many of these changes are being brought about by automation, population mobility, urbanization, national defense, social, economic, and political conditions, as well as by a host of other reasons. As public schools seek to adjust to the needs of society and the needs of pupils, decisions must be made in light of systematically collected and carefully studied data. To help the public comprehend the need for change in the public schools, administrators must involve the public in some type of planning that helps them to recognize this need if the pressing problems of the local school systems are to be met.

A study of social class differences by Celia B. Stendler[14] surveyed the attitudes toward school of parents who had children in the first grade. She found no significant differences in criticisms directed toward the school by social class, although, generally, children from the lower socio-economic classes had received less direct preparation for school and were less likely to have attended a preschool. A similar class differential was found in the degree of expectations and educational aspirations held for the child. The lower-class families seemed to attach little importance to the report card while upper-class families were more likely to accept the report (although with reservations) and to hold higher standards for the child. This study suggests that the child who comes from the lower-class family begins school with fewer advantages than the child from the upper-class family, in part because his parent's attitude toward school is conditioned to a large extent by his socio-economic status.

School program and instructional methods. Many authorities in the field of education agree that all the experiences which children have under the direction of the school may be called curriculum. The basic purpose of school administration is to serve the program and instructional needs of youth. Of couse, many detailed chores are necessary on the part of administrators in order to carry out this basic purpose satisfactorily. What is to be taught and how it is to be taught are important issues that have been with public school people for many decades. For the manner in which the public thinks of education is determined to some extent by what they know

---

[14] Celia B. Stendler, "Social Class Differences in Parental Attitudes Toward School at Grade I Level," *Child Development,* XXII (February, 1951), 37–46.

about it. When changes are about to be made in any phase of the school program or in methodology, one must always ask himself, "What does this do to the school program and to instruction?" Despite the quantity and quality of knowledge in these areas needed by citizens, we have little evidence that many citizens are informed to the extent desirable for most effective judgments about school matters.

In studying published lay opinion on educational programs and problems, Bortner[15] found laymen to be more interested in instructional functions than technical problems of organization. He also found that laymen generally favor curricular content and teaching techniques geared to current conditions and present needs. They favor functional types of instructional programs.

Carter's study of voters and their schools[16] revealed that voters felt schools do a poor job of teaching about budgeting and money, and give too little attention to vocational and psychological guidance. Parents send their children to school to learn; consequently, they seek ways of deciding for themselves whether or not progress has been what they expected. Children grow up and become adults themselves, and many marry and produce children of their own. Many of the feelings held by parents about schools are passed on to their offspring. It is mandatory that school public relations programs work toward helping the many publics understand the school program and how it is carried out.

Structural and Functional Aspects of Community Living that Affect the Understanding of the Schools

Through the years man has learned that the development of his personality as well as of his social group can most likely be achieved through community living. The history of mankind is one of living together. Communities are formed when the varied interests of individuals and families merge for purposes of protection, preservation of culture, or a basic sharing of services. To understand the community one must have knowledge of its past experiences and interests.

Community life may be observed through its form or expression.

---

15 Bortner, *op. cit.*, p. 645.
16 Carter, *op. cit.*, pp. 244–49.

It may express itself through church relationships, family clans, or political adherence to one party or creed. The controlling mode of community expression may rest also with a multiplicity of factors which include domineering individuals and structures.

Communities are quite different from each other. They may consist of large cities, small towns, rural, urban, or suburban areas. These communities may be well organized or they may be poorly organized. In some instances there may be communities within communities. Whatever the conditions, interests are usually common to some degree.

Structural composition. In order to understand community life it is necessary to comprehend the structure of community. Structure, as applied to community, relates to all the essential functions by which a local population maintains itself, and to their interrelations. In view of man's inevitable dependence on his fellows, it appears that the effective unit of the community is not the individual but some combination of individuals. Despite the large range of variability, the human community retains a sufficient consistency of pattern in different times and places to permit its identification as such. Each community has some type of structure. A community may be described in terms of its geographical location, its form of government, its occupations, its historical past, its face-to-face contacts, and its centers of interest. Every community has certain types of interdependence, dependence, and political authority. All of these factors contribute toward a degree of homogeneity.

The school administrator needs to understand the community structure, its dependence and interdependence, and its political authority. These understandings are helpful to an administrator in deciding what facts about schools need communicating to the public, in selecting communications media, and in choosing the personnel to assist in organizing and disseminating public information.

Community groups. It is obvious that the educational administrator who uses modern practices must work with other persons in the formation and development of educational public relations programs. In any democratic action there must be groups, and these may be of many types. At one extreme there is the forum—a loosely formed organization comprising all who want to be members. At the other extreme there is the secret society, in which membership is strictly regulated.

It is imperative that efficient school administrators be informed concerning community groups. According to the National Conference of Professors of Educational Administration,[17] every administrator must know what groups exist in his community. He should know how to discover them. He ought to know how each of them gets its work done. They are of all descriptions—from the highly organized groups of long standing to the loosely formed temporary group whose members have little feeling of solidarity. The nature and function of various groups play an important part in public relations. More than two hundred organizations have been identified as seeking to influence the schools; some of them even go so far as to try to control textbooks and teaching in regard to economic, political, and social questions. Such organizations include patriotic groups, religious and racial groups, business and labor groups, communist, fascist, socialist, and many other political groups.

It is desirable that school administrators become aware of groups that are attempting to influence education and that, through cooperative efforts and good leadership, they direct these influences into the channel that is best for children. First, these groups must be identified.

Public opinion polls or community surveys may reveal facts about groups that are otherwise hidden. Many of these so-called hidden facts determine beliefs, attitudes, and actions of groups. The more information about groups that is brought to light, the better the opportunities for understanding community living. This was brought out by Bardwell[18] who studied the needs and desires of special groups, including the family, farmer, labor, business, manufacturing, professional, civic, recreational, and religious groups. The extent to which the public schools can satisfy the wants and desires of these various groups has considerable effect on the attitudes of the members composing them. He found labor to be the most liberal group in support of education—even more liberal than educators themselves.

How the community is structured and stratified into the groups which get its business done is of utmost importance to the admin-

---

17 National Conference of Professors of Education Administration, *Educational Leaders—Their Functions and Preparation* (Second Work Conference, 1948).

18 R. W. Bardwell, "Measuring Lay Attitudes Toward Education" (Unpublished doctoral dissertation, University of Wisconsin, 1939).

istrator. One of his most important techniques, therefore, is the study of his community in terms of its groups.

Community Use of School Facilities

Within recent years there has been a great increase in the use of school facilities for a wide variety of community purposes. Schools that are responsive to community needs follow many patterns of cooperation with organized groups. This is necessary because of the wide variety in the number and type of organization found in the different communities, and because of differences in relationships between them. Schools may often capitalize on a cordial and cooperative relationship with community agencies. Overlapping objectives and services on the part of agencies should be regarded as an additional resource for youth training, rather than as a basis for rivalry.

Uses of school property. Once again the school is becoming the center of community life. School buildings are being opened for the use of the general public during the evenings and at other times when it will not hinder the work of the regular pupils. Besides being used by adult classes, the school plant is being used as a meeting place for many associations, clubs, societies, and other organizations. A few of the groups that make frequent use of the plant are parent-teacher associations, mothers' clubs, American Red Cross, community clubs, social service federations, welfare associations, farm bureaus, granges, Boy Scouts, Girl Scouts, and chambers of commerce. To this list of the types of organizations which have made use of school property one can add athletic associations, Camp Fire Girls, churches, civic organizations, drum corps, high school clubs, lecture courses, war veterans, political groups, and teachers' clubs.

Community use of the school plant brings a large portion of the public into direct contact with the plant and makes it more necessary than ever that the plant be of such a nature as to inspire respect. A beautiful and well kept plant will inspire greater respect than will one that is not beautiful or well kept.

Rules and regulations. If the community is to use the school plant, there must be rules and regulations to govern such use. School boards should adopt written rules and regulations which are to be followed in permitting the community to use school property. Such policies should give definite methods of securing permission to use the property, the conditions of use, and the fees, if any, which must be paid for the use.

A set of rules and regulations reduces to routine much of the work of letting school property, and gives greater assurance that all groups of the community will be treated equally. Without such guides, school officials are likely to be accused of partiality, and friction will be fostered.

Undoubtedly the public schools are taking on more and more of the nature of community educational centers. Activities which express the desires of the people of a community for their educational, social, and cultural advancement must be recognized.

Legal restrictions.   There are existing legal restrictions which regulate the use of school buildings for other than school purposes. Nearly all of the states have laws that pertain to community use of the school buildings. Within these limitations, and in states that have no such legislation, the discretionary powers reside in the local school board, as the keeper of school property, to grant the use of the public school buildings for purposes other than those directly pertaining to public school.

In educational administration it has commonly been held that public school property is merely held in trust for the state by local authorities, and that the legislature may authorize its use for any purpose not prohibited by the Constitution. Since education is a state function and local plants are purchased through the use of public tax powers, the control of the state is great. There are so many conflicting opinions and state statutes on the use of public school property that conclusions are difficult to draw. The state statutes as well as the courts are divided as to the use of school property for such purposes as staging carnivals or shows, religious exercise, social, fraternal, and political meetings, private or public dances, public assemblies, social gatherings, and similar purposes. In the absence of constitutional or statutory limitations or court decisions to the contrary, discretionary power resides in the local board of education. However, boards of education should not permit the use of school property for private gain, for any purposes which are in any way undesirable for the major purposes intended, or for purposes contrary to the spirit of education.

The author recently had an opportunity to observe a school board and superintendent of a district which asked its solicitor and legal advisor if a particular parochial school could use the public school football field for a major game. The superintendent was advised that it was permissable and granted the use of the field. About two weeks later another parochial school, representing a different religious faith, asked to use the public school football field for an important game and was denied. People in the community surrounding the public school district, including many of the parents who had pupils in the particular public school, became very upset at the disparity in treatment. The superintendent is now being dismissed by the board, and the last school board election saw three new members elected. The superintendent and board members who were replaced believe that the inconsistency in dealing with outside groups concerning the use of school facilities was a contributing factor to their removal.

School Use of Community Resources

The community and the school hold some common responsibilities for the education of their children. A school program that meets the needs of an individual in a democratic society will make use of the resources of the community in which it is located, for when the school works with the society, it can use their combined resources to develop better understandings for the children. The school should be given a chance to observe and work on projects in the community. It is necessary at this point to explore the types of community resources available and the ways and means of using them to improve public relations.

Types of community resources. A community resource is used here to mean anything in the community outside the schools that has educative value and is within the scope of school use. These resources may be represented by institutions, services, materials, and processes. Community resources with education as an objective may provide services of a distributive, vocational, social, citizenship, leisure, cultural, agricultural, health, and guidance nature. Some examples of community resources for classroom use are listed in a bulletin which is published by the curriculum office of the school district of Philadelphia[19] and addressed to the principals of schools

---

[19] Curriculum Office, *Community Resources for Classroom Use* (Philadelphia Public Schools: Services of the Community Educational Relationships Office, 1963).

having grades seven and eight. This booklet contains more than thirty-five community resources for classroom use and the blanks through which the services may be requested. A sample of the resources listed include American Institute of Banking, Bar Association, Family Service of Philadelphia, City Council, City Hall, Common Pleas Court, Federal Bureau of Investigation, Lankenau Health Museum, Municipal Speakers Bureau, and the World Affairs Council.

At this point it is wise to ask what kinds of community experiences are useful. Olsen[20] lists twenty kinds of community activities involving observation, participation, and contribution, some of the most significant of which are: map the community area, study the sources of community income, survey the community's public opinion structure and processes, become acquainted with minority groups and leaders, study community agencies, and make a comprehensive community survey.

It is recognized that variations will exist among community resources in the emphasis placed upon the various objectives. Different community resources emphasize various activities and services in the attainment of their objectives. But in almost all cases, first-hand study of community resources permits the student to see the practice of some useful skills that he has studied and heard about in school. All the patterns of life, past and present, as well as the physical facilities of the community, are valuable resources. In the concept of the modern school we use the business officials, municipal activities, service agencies, and clubs as part of our classroom.

One of the most important ingredients in the effectiveness of a school is for the teacher to know the needs and resources of his community so that he can make an intelligent application of them to his classroom instructional program. In order to implement any program based on the resources of the community, the teachers must also have a knowledge of his own pupils, their interests, abilities, and differences.

Nature and procedures.   Commonly used procedures or techniques for the utilization of community resources include contests, lectures, interviews, map and graph construction, school trips, sur-

---

[20] Edward G. Olsen, *School and Community,* 2nd ed. (Englewood Cliffs, N.J.: Prentice-Hall, Inc., 1957), pp. 121–22.

veys, and work experiences. Not all of the procedures listed here are used by all segments of the teaching profession.

All too few schools at present use their community resources to good advantage in their educational program. In many cases such use is limited almost entirely to visits by classroom groups to points of interest within the community—for instance, to a museum or a park—and often little attempt has been made to make such a trip a real experience or to bring to the school those people in the community with real and vital experience of interest to the student.

One may find educators today who think that school studies must come first and foremost, and that if community experiences is to have a part, it must be a very small and secondary one. On the other side of the picture we find some who are aware of the necessity of community experience, and would place its importance above that of school studies. Their reasoning is based on a knowledge that the student has a great deal of difficulty coping with his school studies, which often have no basis in real life, whereas the use of the resources of the community puts him in touch with something he has had contact with and is meaningful to him. The community experiences provided for pupils should be at the levels of observing, participating, and planning for the future. However, any one of these levels by itself is not enough; we must use all three in developing in the pupil a sense of responsibility for the improvement of the community in which he lives. Some authorities in education say that the pupil need not be limited to his own community, but can even go to other states or countries to broaden his knowledge. Their reasoning is based on the fact that through improved means of transportation and communication our world is growing relatively smaller and becoming more of a community in itself. As students learn about their communities, "feedback" to school and community leaders begins to take place and opportunities for mutual understanding are enhanced. An additional avenue is created which provides for better school community relations.

CHAPTER III

Organization and Administration

Need and Types of Organization

The public relations service of the school system definitely should be organized and systematized, just as every other school service should be organized and systematized. Unless definite plans are made, this important service is likely to be of a hit or miss variety or to be entirely neglected. Incidental public relations activities are apt to be accidental. The direction of public relations efforts must be channeled and organized to produce optimum beneficial results to the school and to the society it serves. An organization and systematization of the service is needed whether the school system is large or small. Personnel should be carefully selected, and provision should be made for necessary community contacts and financial support. The organization of the public relations service and its administration should be in keeping with its dignity as a major administrative function.

Need for organization. The nature of the organization depends upon the prevailing philosophy and policy concerning public relations. The nature of the policy will help determine the personnel to be selected and the program to be adopted. Unless both philosophy and policy are carefully thought through, the organization may become a haphazard affair. Schools vary in their relationships in carrying on public school relations. To achieve effective results all schools should have definite philosophies, goals, objectives, and patterns or organization.

While a successful public relations program is considered a key to a better educational program, organized programs are far from universal; finding a special set-up for the administration of public relations programs is not the pattern in the typical school system. Many programs of public relations consist largely of publicity practices planned and executed by the professional personnel in the various school units. A great need exists for a functional plan of public school relations which features effective programs of institutional and community interpretation.

Authorities agree that some form of organization is needed regardless of the size of the system, the character of the community, or its attitude toward the school. Most researches point out the definite need for greater attention to be given to administrative organization and procedures in public relations. It is imperative that public relations programs be planned and formulated in order to render continuous service and contacts.

Accepted types of organization. The organization of an effective public relations program is the essential foundation upon which its success in carrying out its desired objectives is based. Although, for one reason or another, few authors have attempted to spell out types of organization that have been found effective in public relations programs, there is some agreement that there are three general types of organization in current use. These are: (1) a centralized plan; (2) a decentralized plan; and (3) a coordinate plan. The centralized plan places the responsibility for the program with the chief administrative officer and his immediate line and staff personnel. The decentralized plan places the responsibility for the program with the building principal and his staff. The coordinate plan combines features from both of the others.

Research studies relating to this topic are almost nonexistent. The most significant study dealing with types of organization for public relations is rather old, but it is national in scope and provides some detailed guidelines. In a study of the direction of public relations in the United States, John M. Hickey[1] found six types of organization. For the purpose of clarity, a more detailed description of each type of organization will be presented in the paragraphs that follow.

Superintendent of schools. The superintendent of schools is the director of public relations as well as the chief administrative officer of the school system. The superintendent keeps in close contact with parents and citizens on the one hand, and with various community groups on the other. He directs a program which includes the board of education, staff officers, principals, teachers, pupils, and non-professional employees all working together directly or indirectly with the two groups mentioned above. Specific tasks or duties may be

---

[1] John M. Hickey, "The Direction of Public Relations in Cities of the United States" (Unpublished doctoral dissertation, University of Pittsburgh, 1945), p. 319.

given to one person or a committee under the superintendent to make the program function.

One distinct advantage of this type of organization is that the superintendent of schools is the most prominent of the school officials and will be known to many laymen who are acquainted with no one else in the school system. He is generally regarded as the top school leader and educational authority in the community.

Administrative staff officer.   In this type of organization the administrative staff officer is the director of the public relations program and is responsible to the superintendent for the program. He works with the parent, citizen, and community group categories as did the superintendent in the first type. He may serve as director of research, director of curriculum, or in some similar function, but in any case one of his major functions will be to coordinate all public relations activities.

Director of public school relations.   Several of the larger cities such as Denver, Detroit, New York, Oakland, Los Angeles, Cincinnati, and Kansas City have a director of public relations on a full-time basis. He may have one or more staff assistants as well as a full-time secretary. He is responsible to the superintendent of schools and must be a person well qualified to direct the program. He must have a good academic background and professional experience in school administration as well as a specialized training in the principles and techniques of public relations. In addition, he should possess writing and speaking ability, tactfulness, a sense of humor, and a sense of proportion.

The building principal.   In this type of organization the school principal directs the program. The building principal type of organization has been successful in Chicago, Illinois, Lawrence Park, Pennsylvania, and Tampa, Florida. This system puts the director close to the educational activities and the individuals who make contact with the community—namely, the teachers, students, and parents—through visitation, parent-teacher associations, and other miscellaneous contacts. The principal in charge of the program works through the administrative staff but does the organizing for public relations.

Decentralized principal.   The most popular type of organization found is the decentralized principal type where each principal directs a program for his school. Each principal is, of course, responsible to the superintendent of schools and the board of education. At his own discretion he can form committee groups of teachers and students in order to carry out the various programs to develop and further school-community relations.

Teacher committee. This type of organization has teacher committees in charge of public school relations. In a large school district with two or more secondary schools, each school would have a teacher committee to organize and carry out the program. The committees work in cooperation with the superintendent, principals, other teachers, and students in executing sound relations with the parents, citizens, and the community at large. Some cities which have used this type of organization are Birmingham, Alabama, New Castle, Pennsylvania, and Oklahoma City, Oklahoma.

Responsibilities of the School Board

The United States Constitution delegates the responsibility for education to the various states under the Tenth Amendment. In the early days of this country the local communities were in complete control of education since both the colonial charters and the state constitutions omitted references to education.[2] It was assumed that the individual communities could best determine and meet the educational needs of the populace. It was soon discovered that the communities tended to avoid educational responsibilities and that leaving educational decisions entirely in the hands of the local community resulted in the neglect of this implied function. States then began to pass laws and to write into their constitutions minimal educational requirements. The early state laws concerning education tended to require towns to establish schools. As the towns increased in complexity, the power of the town meetings were delegated to selectmen who provided for the maintenance of teachers and education. As the problems of overseeing schools became more complex, the selectmen found it necessary to delegate the responsibility for schools to special committees. These committees were charged with seeing that the state-assigned educational functions were carried out.

In the early nineteenth century the states began to assume more

---

[2] Edwin H. Smith, "An Evaluation of the School Board Policy Manuals of Selected Urban School Districts in Ten Southeastern States" (Unpublished doctoral dissertation, University of Miami, 1962), pp. 10–12.

and more control over educational matters while delegating responsibility to the school boards and districts. The early pattern of school committees or school boards which was established in New England spread with the southern and westward movements and became the accepted means through which the states carried out their educational functions.

Today a school board possesses large powers assigned to it by constitutional and statutory law and has vast discretion extending beyond the limits of legal provisions. Most often the board makes the final financial decisions which decide the scope of the educational program and services.

The school board occupies a unique and strategic position in school public relations. The men and women who serve on boards are laymen, chosen and selected by one manner or another to represent the people. These people are duty bound to formulate policy, to interpret and decide issues in the best interest of the community, to provide for financing the educational needs of the community, to report on the progress and operations of the schools, to employ a superintendent of schools, and to exercise judicial functions. The board of education defines the powers, duties, and responsibilities of the superintendent but does not tell him how to do his job. These general duties of the board are well known, but their less well known responsibilities are those associated with public relations. In the paragraphs that follow the school board's specific public relations responsibilities will be defined and discussed.[3]

Head the educational system. Although education is considered a function and responsibility of the state through legislative enactment and delegated authority, the board of education stands at the head of our educational program. This principle is supported by the fact that the basic character of public education in the United States is, in the final analysis, determined by the board that controls the policies and finances of the said school system. To a large extent, and in a manner seldom understood by the public, the content and purpose of public education will reflect the quality of the membership of the school board. A board functions best when its role is restricted to the functions previously outlined and when it leaves the administration of the system to the superintendent and his staff.

---

[3] Some of the material presented in this section is used by permission from Warwick & York, Inc., Baltimore, Maryland, publishers of *Educational Administration and Supervision.*

The public school boards of America are organized in their several State School Boards Associations, and federated into the National School Boards Association, Inc. In a statement of beliefs and policies which the National School Boards Association, adopted in 1956 comes the following excerpt concerning public relations in public education:

> The National School Boards Association recognizes that underlying every problem of public education—is the problem of how to enlist the understanding and support of the American Public as a whole. When people are accused of apathy toward the schools, it is usually because they do not know the facts regarding school conditions, needs, and potentialities.[4]

Universal public education will best serve the strength and welfare of our nation and its people if the board can accept the principle that it owes allegiance only to the welfare of all children and youth. The success of any school system and its staff is reflected in the confidence the board has in its administration and in the relations that are built up with the community.

Orient and educate new members. The membership of the typical board of education shifts rapidly. Old members retire and new ones are added through proper election or appointment. The process of study and understanding is therefore continuous. School board members must be well informed if they are to help evaluate school programs and to be able to answer questions concerning vital problems relative to pupil needs, local, state, and national control. New school board members desperately need to know the conditions of the schools and the needs and conditions of the community in which the school system operates. It is imperative that a training program be provided for new board members. Despite the fact that the superintendent often plays a major role in the training of new members, the board of education and the state board's association should think of the orientation process of school board members as part of their responsibility.

An example of a type of orientation program found to be helpful to new board members is the annual workshop conducted by the Virginia School Boards Association for new members at the University of Virginia.[5] The workshop is planned by the program com-

---

[4] National School Boards Association, Inc., *Yearbook* (Chicago: The Association, 1958), p. 30.

[5] The writer served as Executive Secretary of the Virginia State School Boards Association for two years—1956–1957.

mittee of the state association in cooperation with the Executive Secretary, who is also a member of the University faculty. Both experienced board members and superintendents, along with members of the State Department of Education, provide incidents, experiences, short cases, and other issues for discussion. The new members are supplied a series of pamphlets, books, school board manuals, and samples of problems confronting boards. Public relations problems constitute almost one half of the situations studied. Board members are given the opportunity of practicing without worrying about making mistakes at the expense of school districts in the course of learning through errors made on the job. These workshops have been well received and thought worthwhile by new board members.

A comprehensive list of twenty-five suggestions for new school board members was prepared by W. A. Shannon[6] and published by the National School Boards Association. This list ranges from reviewing special reports to attending at board meetings as a guest before actually becoming a board member. Almost all of his suggestions have implications for public relations.

It is essential for the well being of the schools that the new school board member be accepted as a part of the board as soon as possible and that the board gradually and intelligently orient him into the pattern of group activity.

A board that takes planned action to educate its members certainly provides a method for the promotion of good public relations between the school and its community.

Report to the public.   The board of education is a body incorporate which owes its existence to the state, derives its legal authority therefrom, and is responsible to the people for the maintenance of a program of education in accordance with general approval. Today some twenty-three states have legal statutes requiring the school boards to report to the people on the conditions of the schools at regular intervals. Failure of boards of education to present and interpret pertinent facts about the school system has been responsible for much public misunderstanding of the educational program and its related activities. People who lack complete and accurate information often form judgments which are not accurate and may be prejudicial to the school. Since the schools belong to the public, it

---

[6] W. A. Shannon, "Suggestions for the New School Board Member," *Yearbook* (Chicago: National School Boards Association, 1957), pp. 110–11.

is the responsibility of the board to be well enough informed to clear up misunderstandings and to promote public relations through the kind of data they give the public.

Some of the types of information that boards may provide to the public include written school board policies, superintendents' annual reports (printed for public consumption), printed reports on matters of special interest to parents, bulletins and publications addressed to the general public and to citizens who do not have children in school, newsletters, and interschool house organs for teachers, board members, and organization leaders. In addition boards may provide radio and television broadcasts and tape recordings. Special public hearings in which the audience may respond may be held on crucial issues. It would be well for the board members to remember that they are elected officials and that they have a duty to consult with the taxpayers and to identify the school product which the tax dollar buys.

In a modern school system with a functional public relations organization, the superintendent will see that the legislative body is provided a constant flow of information. Each member should be aware of the exact condition of the school system and should be thoroughly acquainted with its needs.

Exchange information and ideas with the school executive.   It should be remembered that the school board can inform the superintendent of many desires of the people of the community. There are activities in every school organization which present ample opportunities for discharging the dual obligations of interpretation between the superintendent and the school board. Since each school presents a different situation, no specific formula can be given whereby a superintendent and a school board may have a universal rule of procedure in reciprocally interpreting the things of importance concerning the school and the community. However, an excellent opportunity for the school board and the executive to exchange information is the school board meeting. The functions of a board cannot be legally performed except in a regular or special board meeting; a school board must transact all its business in such a meeting. No matter how urgent or how trivial a matter may be, the board cannot handle the case without meeting as a body and taking regular action. A board cannot legally act by each member merely giving his consent, one at his factory, another at his office, one at his grocery, another at his home. When the board is not in session there is legally *no board*. The proper conduct of all meetings is therefore a matter of utmost importance.

Every board of education should operate as a board rather than as individuals. This can be done officially only in regular meetings provided by law or in such special meetings as may be required.

Hold open and informal meetings to obtain citizen reactions. The board of education is in a special position to hold informal meetings and to obtain citizen reactions. It is legally designated as that part of the public responsible for being best informed about the schools. Through the board the public frequently exercises its responsibility for determining school aims and results. School board meetings are legally open to the public except for executive sessions. Not only should most meetings be open to the public but they should also invite the press and give it sufficient materials to enable it to carry full reports to the public.

School boards have learned that a good form of protection against pressure groups and special interests is a well informed public. They have learned that their worst critics, and the worst critics of the school program, are the uninformed, and that the best way to convert an opponent into an ardent supporter of the schools is to put him to work gathering information about the schools and helping to plan needed improvements in the school program.[7]

Some school districts provide opportunities through open meetings for citizens to present requests, ideas, and complaints directly to the board. Having the board serve as an audience to citizen reactions is one way of securing general public opinion concerning innovations and practices the district may wish to initiate. Topics having popular appeal and discussed in several states include the need for junior colleges at public expense, a new type of vocational training, and the teaching of newer mathematics.

One of the specific responsibilities of the local school board is the interpretation of the community it represents to the professional group and the interpretation of the professional group to the community. To act as a liaison between the professional group on the one hand and the social group on the other, the board of education must understand both the community and the schools.

[7] Book excerpt, "How to Get Your Public's Support," *School Management,* VI, No. 104, April, 1962.

Through his many contacts the board member also receives much gossip and much distorted information from members of the community. If thoroughly informed, he may counteract these situations by presenting the facts quietly and effectively and offering reference to them in published form. Since the board member hears many things that seldom if ever come to the professional ear, his community contacts form an invaluable part of any interpretative program, both as a corrective and as a reporting agent.

Utilize the professional staff in developing broad policies for the public relations program. Since it is generally accepted that one of the basic duties of a school board is to determine all school policy, it is its responsibility to establish policy in regard to public relations. Generally this policy, like other policies of the board, would be recommended by the superintendent of schools and his co-workers. One authority[8] in this field makes it clear that a primary function of the board is to delegate to the chief executive officer and his staff the job of translating the public relations policy into a practical program. This often involves the practice of inviting several members of the professional staff to meet with the board and the administrative staff in order to make suggestions concerning the development of public relations policy. The personnel invited are usually those persons who have special skills or training in areas such as journalism, English, radio, television, and speech. The training and experience of the professional staff can add immeasurably to policy development in this area when given the opportunity. The board represents the general community and must not let autocracy prevail in the control of educational affairs. The thinking of the professionals can be of tremendous assistance in aiding broad policy development in regard to public relations.

Appraise public opinion. An implied subsidiary responsibility is the evaluation of public opinion as expressed by organized groups. In most walks of American life people join organized groups in which they share common interests, goals, or ideals with fellow members. Several of these groups manifest a genuine interest in the public schools while others seek directly or indirectly to impose their wishes upon the schools. This latter group may be referred to as a pressure group. It may use lobbying, speakers' bureaus, youth move-

---

[8] Leslie W. Kindred, *School Public Relations* (Englewood Cliffs, N.J.: Prentice-Hall, Inc., 1957), p. 406.

ments, or printed materials to influence the school toward its own goals which may be in conflict with the values held by the school. Of course, not all pressure groups work in opposition to public education. The board must ultimately distinguish between those groups that seek to serve their own interests and those that earnestly want to help the schools. Boards will want to cooperate with many public and voluntary agencies.

A friendly attitude toward groups concerned with leisure time or avocational interests should prevail, and the board should grant and encourage use of the school facilities by outside groups whenever possible. Above all, it should be the duty of school authorities to get the idea across to the public that the public relations program is largely concerned with promoting the interest of pupils rather than the special interests of school personnel, pressure groups, or others who wish to advance selfish goals.

It is important that the school board, through its superintendent, determine the type and nature of organized groups to be found in the community, what their purposes are, and how they are interrelated. This process will probably make use of reports, surveys, opinion studies, and other types of data gathering referred to in an earlier section with reference to understanding the community.

Provide the means for interpretation. Although interpretations of the community to professional groups and of professional groups to the community are important, they are not the board's sole duty, for it also has a responsibility for helping make available the money and finances necessary to carry out a program of interpretation. Likewise, the board of education needs to provide the media for keeping the community informed of the purpose, value, conditions, and needs of its schools.

Boards of education must decide the kinds of reports and publicity that shall be given the work of the public schools. Accompanying this decision must be some type of annual appropriation for these reports. It may be that annual reports, semi-annual reports, or monthly reports will be made to the public of school activities. The means for interpretation may involve radio, press releases, television, or the making of school movies. Whatever the means for explaining the school to the public, they must be understood and plans must be made for their implementation.

Express policies and defend the action of the school. As an individual, a board member has no legal authority. Two of his responsibilities lie in furnishing the people with facts about the actual conditions, and in discovering and reporting conflicts to the executive. Wherever the school board member goes, he should consciously strive to keep open all available contacts and to utilize them for giving reliable information about the schools as well as for ascertaining the attitudes of the people toward the schools. By virtue of his position in the community and the groups to which he belongs, the board member has access to representatives from audiences that no superintendent or teacher can reach, and because of this situation particular emphasis should be given this phase of the public relations program.

It appears evident that the individual members of the board of education should be thoroughly conversant with the problems confronting education, because they have many opportunities to express the policies and defend the action of the school. Because of their participation in the various community groups, the school board members are in position to influence favorable public opinion toward the school through an attitude of informed, straightforward dissemination of facts regarding the school. In some districts it appears that this important function of the school board either has been overlooked or given inadequate attention by those responsible for the school's public relations program. More related data concerning this point will be presented in connection with the responsibilities of the superintendent as portions of the research cover both areas.

Responsibilities of the Superintendent

Virtually every new function accepted by the school carries with it the need for understanding and cooperation by the school personnel and community forces. The administrator's role in improving school-community ties has become more significant and certainly more difficult over the years.[9] Since 1900, the administrator's concept of his job in this area has shifted from "indifference" to "publicity campaigns" to "educational interpretation" to "cooperative

[9] Gene C. Fusco, "Implications for School-Community Relations of Psychological Studies in Communication," in *Communications Research And School-Community Relations* (Cooperative Research Project, No. G–037 of the U.S. Office of Education, College of Education, Temple University, Philadelphia, 1965), p. 174.

endeavor" or the "school-community partnership."[10] This latter concept views the school as a social institution which moves forward as an integrated process. It takes into consideration new discoveries concerning teaching and child development. These changing concepts concerning the role of the superintendent in public relations have made more critical the relationship between the superintendent's success on the job and his competency in developing effective public relations programs.

In a summary of the research conducted through the Cooperative Project in Educational Administration which was supported by the W. K. Kellog Foundation, Hollis Moore[11] cites more than thirty studies concerning the relationship of the school to the community. Despite the fact that these studies raised more questions than they answered, it was made abundantly clear that the school administrator needs to improve his competencies in public relations.

A survey of superintendents conducted by the American Association of School Administrators in 1960 indicated that superintendents are concerned about their competencies in public relations. Almost 4,000 administrators in towns and cities with populations of 2,500 or more responded to the Association's questionnaire.[12] Among the courses listed as being helpful and important in advanced graduate study, public relations was ranked third—just below finance and curriculum. What is more, superintendents ranked public relations fifth in a list of eighteen weaknesses they reported.

Further evidence of the significance of public relations to the success of the superintendent on the job is indicated by a survey of all chief state school officers and all executive secretaries of the state teacher associations conducted by Richard B. Kennan[13] of the NEA's National Commission on Professional Rights and Responsibilities. Kennan sought to secure his subjects' opinions as to why superintendents get fired. Both the state secretaries and the state superintendents agreed that the most frequently mentioned factor (other

10 James J. Jones and Irving W. Stout, *School Public Relations: Issues and Cases* (New York: G. P. Putnam's Sons), pp. 6–9.

11 Hollis A. Moore, Jr., *Studies in School Administration* (Washington, D.C.: American Association of School Administrators, 1957).

12 American Association of School Administrators, *Profile of the School Superintendent* (Washington, D.C.: The Association, 1960).

13 Richard B. Kennan, "Why They Got Fired," Speech delivered at the American Association of School Administrator's Regional Convention in Atlantic City, N.J., 1961 (mimeographed), p. 2.

than incompetence) preventing success of superintendents is poor public relations.

An extensive study of the school superintendency in Massachusetts was made by Neal Gross[14] who gathered information through personal interviews in order to develop a thorough analysis of the job of the school superintendent in terms of community social structure. He discovered that only 40 per cent of the school board members rated their superintendent excellent in the area of public relations.

To a large degree the quality of leadership determines the success of the public relations program. In order to provide the necessary leadership, the superintendent may organize and delegate many public relations responsibilities. The following responsibilities are found to be most effective in the work of the superintendent of schools.[15]

Organizing the machinery. Organized leadership for public relations provides the basis for successful school-community initiative in meeting the educational needs of children. Lack of an organized program of public relations may cause a patron to form his opinion of the entire school system from the result of a single experience. While every school system should have some form of organization for public relations, actual organized programs are far from universal. They are found principally in large administrative units. Where public relations programs are definitely organized, the superintendent of schools is most often the key figure in the organization. The school's chief executive officer is the person responsible for the public relations program. The basic machinery needed by a school to do an acceptable job in school-community understanding usually exists in every school district. The superintendent is responsible to the board of education for all phases of the conduct of the schools. It is his task to organize the machinery for school-community relations into a unified operation. Through organization the administrator, without relinquishing his responsibility for the program, is able to delegate many public relations functions, and thus find the time to develop a comprehensive program. He should develop the pro-

---

[14] Neal Gross, *Who Runs Our Schools?* (New York: John Wiley Sons, Inc., 1958).

[15] For additional detail, *see* James J. Jones, "Organize for Better Public Relations," *Phi Delta Kappan,* XXXIV (February, 1953), 164, 167.

gram of school-community relations cooperatively, as any autocratic efforts are likely to be futile.

Providing leadership and interpretation. Interpretation is the proper function of the superintendent. He is responsible for the development, as an integral part of the program, of the educational philosophy, policy, and program of the school system, especially as these relate to school-community relations. Where the impetus comes from outside the school, he should cooperate fully if the proposed plan or organization can help the program. The superintendent must lead the movement to bring the public to see the over-all objectives and to give meaning to the many parts of the entire school program. He must see that each activity is explainable in the light of its association with the total process. As leader of staff and teachers he should encourage every person connected with the schools to participate effectively in the publicity programs adopted. The school administrator must be a leader who can inspire the staff, teachers, and patrons to community study and community interpretation, and who can assist in explaining the changing program of the school system. Leadership in the superintendent involves the ability to guide the activities of others and to get them to cooperate.

Informing the board of education. Most authorities agree that informing the board of education on all phases of school work is a major responsibility of the superintendent of schools. If school board members are to intelligently execute the obligation placed upon them, it is essential that they have accurate and reliable information on all phases of the school's work. Most, if not all, board members have their own vocations to pursue and their private business to conduct; they cannot devote more than a few hours each week to the work of the schools, as they must secure their livelihood from other sources. It is one of the most highly important tasks of the superintendent to present all the facts in a well organized and well arranged manner so that they may be easily understood. This is a task which he cannot neglect, for if he neglects it, the plan and policies which the board adopts are not likely to be the most enlightened ones, and the interests of the school and the public relations program will suffer.

In trying to keep the board members informed, it is usually desirable for the superintendent to help provide the means for this information. Some of the more important of these means are reading, providing a notebook for each member, visiting schools, attending educational conventions, and holding personal conferences.

It is the continuous duty of the superintendent to provide information concerning the work of the schools to the board of education, and to advise it on professional matters.

Analyzing outside demands and pressures. It is necessary that the school administrator study the community and its groups in order to be aware of those groups that influence education. Since all demands are expressions of the will and temper of parts of the public, each demand contributes an opportunity for better knowledge of popular will and temper and for fuller evaluation of them. Even the many demands which are based on incomplete or inaccurate information and interpretation offer the school superintendent opportunities to capitalize the attention and interest of both the demand group and the inactive public, and to build a better understanding of the facts and relationships involved. It is imperative that superintendents understand the nature of outside demands and pressures made on the public schools, and that through careful analysis of these demands, they construct better relations between the respective schools and communities.

Evaluation of the public relations program. Evaluation should be regarded as a highly important and necessary phase of the public relations program. The various activities of the public relations program should be appraised in the light of the objectives and purposes for which they were planned. Responsibility for evaluation of a school public relations program rests with the board of education and the superintendent of schools, with the latter occupying the central position. The actual evaluation may or may not be undertaken by the superintendent himself. In most instances he will inevitably participate in any program of evaluation and must accept responsibility for what is done, although others are designated or employed for that purpose. He should use every opportunity to confer with laymen, individual citizens, parents, and other community groups, in order to properly appraise the program. It must be remembered that the public is indirectly appraising the program in many ways. A more detailed description of evaluation is presented in Chapter VII.

CHAPTER IV

The Staff and Public Relations

Director of Public Relations

More and more school districts are employing people with special training to head their public relations programs. School superintendents and boards of education are becoming increasingly aware of the special skills needed to explain the school to the community and to compete successfully with other mass media for citizen understanding and interest.

Need for a director. All school districts need a public relations program, but the way in which individual systems go about organizing to meet this need varies widely. In the small school district a portion of the teacher's time and effort may be set aside and used to inform the public about the school and its work. When the school district is large, it is often economical and efficient to delegate and to assign the organization and administration of the public relations program to a specialized person in the central office. Whether the public relations program is organized on an attendance unit level or on an administrative unity level will depend upon the prevailing philosophy of the local school district. In the small or medium sized district, the responsibility for the public relations program can be and often is handled by the superintendent. In the larger districts the superintendent generally selects and appoints an assistant to perform these functions. Many authorities in educational administration suggest that any school district located in a community with a population of 50,000 or more can benefit by the employment of a full-time director of public relations.

Title of the position. Although the title of the position may at first seem unimportant, it proves to be of vital significance in that it describes the relevant responsibilities in very general terms. According to Leslie W. Kindred,[1] who collected data from eighty school

---

[1] Leslie W. Kindred, "Assistant Superintendent—Community Relations," *Preparation Programs for School Administrators* (East Lansing, Michigan: Michigan State University, 1963), p. 207.

systems having a person in charge of public relations, the titles used most frequently are assistant superintendent for public relations, co-ordinator or director of school-community relations, director of public relations, coordinator or supervisor of public information, administrative assistant to the superintendent, director of information services, and director of publications. Irrespective of the title assigned to the person carrying out these responsibilities for the superintendent at the district level, it is imperative that boards of education who seek to establish this position define with extreme care the nature and scope of the functions of the director of public relations.

Functions and responsibilities. Despite the fact that the superintendent may be well qualified to direct and to synchronize the work in public relations, it is questionable that he will have ample time to do this work while still taking care of his other duties and responsibilities. As school systems increase in size and scope, so too does the quantity of work. Therefore, when a position of director of public relations is created, a job description should be developed. The person who occupies this position will need to know precisely what he is expected to do as well as what his relationships with others in the school system are. A position guide makes it easier for the superintendent and local board of education to develop a job description. A recently developed position guide for the director of school-community relations[2] provides eight possible basic functions as follows: (1) establishing and maintaining efficient channels of communication between personnel within the school system; (2) coordinating the public relations activities of all personnel employed by the board of education; (3) providing services on call which contribute either directly or indirectly to the strengthening of school-community relations program; (4) working cooperatively with outside groups and organizations that have constructive interest in public education; (5) undertaking assigned responsibilities in the school-community relations program; (6) involving citizens in the work of the school and in the solving of educational problems; (7) serving as a consultant to the superintendent, and through him to the board of education, on matters involving relationships with the com-

---

[2] Leslie W. Kindred, "Position Guide . . . for Director of School-Community Relations," *Bulletin of the Pennsylvania School Boards Association,* XXVIII (March, 1964), 38–41.

munity; and (8) appraising the effectiveness of the public relations program and making recommendations for its improvement. Despite the breadth and scope of functions listed in the position guide, it is not intended that all directors of public relations perform every function and every responsibility outlined above. Rather, the board may wish to use the position guide as an example, and to select whatever functions it wishes to assign to the director of public relations.

This same position guide lists twenty-nine regular and ten occasional responsibilities, as well as five types of relationship for the director of public relations within the school system. The array of responsibilities range from providing leadership in the planning, organizing, and appraising of the public relations program to keeping the superintendent informed of prevailing public opinion regarding specific policies, practices, and programs of the school system. The relationships of the director to all other personnel are spelled out in six complete steps as follows:[3]

1. Answering directly to the superintendent of schools for the implementation of assigned functions and responsibilities and the degree to which they have been carried out successfully.

2. Reporting directly to the superintendent of schools on the public relations needs, conditions, and problems of the system, and making constructive suggestions for their treatment.

3. Keeping the superintendent informed of prevailing public opinion relative to the school system and of any shifts that occur in attitudes and convictions about specific policies, practices, and programs.

4. Working coordinately and cooperatively with administrative officers below the superintendent of schools on public relations problems and activities for which they have responsibility.

5. Working coordinately and cooperatively with any other individual or group upon a directive from the superintendent of schools.

It is not anticipated that any individual could possibly attempt to perform all the responsibilities and relationships described here without the aid of numerous competent assistants. One way to get the position defined is to decide which of these activities are important to a particular school district and then write a job description that embodies the phases to be covered by the director of public relations.

Characteristics and qualifications. The director of public rela-

---

[3] *Ibid.,* p. 41.

tions will need to be well qualified to assume the functions and responsibilities discussed previously. In far too many instances the duties of public relations directors have been perceived in terms of publicity or informational services. It is strongly recommended that this position be viewed as one that mandates the director to have a broad understanding of professional education and a general acquaintance with the theory and practice of educational administration, and to be sophisticated in the use of the technical skills connected with communication media.

In order to select a person for the position of director of public relations, a school board ought to look for someone who possesses some of the following general characteristics: (1) ability to work with people; (2) capacity to understand the educational field; (3) ability to express ideas in writing; (4) capacity to organize public relations programs; (5) ability to persuade individuals and groups; (6) ability to address an audience; and (7) ability to delegate work to others.[4] It would also be helpful if the director believes in the worth and importance of public education in a democracy and has good mental and physical health.

Administrative Assistants

Included in the classification of administrative assistants are the assistant superintendents, the general and special supervisors, and the directors of special areas or departments. In addition to their routine duties, in which they have daily contact with the public, these persons are often given specific responsibilities calling for the ability to assume unique leadership roles. For example, the assistant superintendent may be asked to be responsible for the use of buildings and grounds and to deal with all non-school groups that wish to use school plant facilities. An assistant superintendent may be charged with the responsibility for business management of the school system and at the same time may be given the additional task of providing printed materials that are to be distributed to the public in regard to the budget process for public relations purposes. The assistant superintendent in charge of personnel may be asked to add selected printed materials to the list that he develops for the recruit-

---

[4] John M. Hickey, "The Direction of Public Relations in Cities of the United States" (Unpublished doctoral dissertation, University of Pittsburgh, 1945).

ment of teachers and other personnel. Likewise, he may be given charge of spot radio and television programs geared to telling the school story in an attractive manner for recruitment and public relations purposes. Many administrative assistants serving in central offices are competent to give special service and to advise in areas of public relations closely related to their own specialties. It is part of the responsibility of the superintendent as well as of the director of public relations to use the talents and skills of the administrative assistants to their fullest extent in promoting public relations.

The Principal's Responsibilities

Organized public relations programs occupy an important place in the administrative phase of our public schools. In planning and carrying out such programs at the local school level, there are many integral parts to be administered and someone needs to assume the responsibility for coordinating the several elements of such programs in each individual school. In the vast majority of our schools this challenge belongs to the principal.

Systematize the machinery. Generally the principal and the staff take part in the over-all program of public relations for the school district and also carry out a special program of interpretation of the school in which they work. It is a part of the principal's job to organize the machinery for public relations within his own school.[5] He is the person who maintains contacts between the school and the community, as well as between the district office and the larger community it serves. To see that a positive program of public relations is developed and administered at the local level is a responsibility that cannot be delegated, as it belongs to the school principal.

Capitalize on personal contacts. One of the most significant acts of the principal concerning public relations is the manner in which he makes use of his personal contacts. In the course of each school day the principal meets and talks with many parents, citizens, and pupils. Rigorous demands are placed upon him and his ability to explain the policies and practices of the school in a manner that can be understood by the public. Some of the principal's time devoted to interpreting the work of the school may involve his appear-

---

[5] James J. Jones, "The Principal and Public Relations," *Educational Administration and Supervision*, XLI (May, 1955), 313–17.

ances at civic and service group functions within the community. Other opportunities to explain the school may come about through conferences with parents who are unhappy or discontented and bring their concerns to the principal. He is the school's agent before the public and is the person most likely to be able to shed light upon problems concerning the school and to advise people with respect to the school's purposes, needs, and opportunities. The principal represents a social institution of immediate concern to the public. As a leader of the local school, the principal has the job of planning, executing, achieving results through the direction and stimulation of others.

Provide a quality educational program. Perhaps the best way to promote a good public relations program is to provide a sound, high quality educational program. Because parents send their children to public schools to be taught, the better the instructional program, the easier it becomes to advance a satisfying program of public relations. An educational program of quality is based upon sound research and effective practices that meet the needs of all pupils, not just of one particular group, such as college-bound students. Parental attitudes about school are conditioned by the success or failure of their children in school. One goal of the well trained principal is likely to be that of helping lift the sights of the community in terms of education. As a community leader, he can do much to lead the community into a cooperative program of community action. The *whole* child goes to school and reacts to his total environment both at school and in the community. Under this concept the school becomes one of the centers of community life. No quantity of publicity can serve as a substitute for quality in the program. The final satisfaction with the value of public education is determined by the satisfaction derived from its program of instruction. A contented child and a satisfied parent form the best combination for understanding the school.

Increase the involvement of others in decision-making. The manner in which a principal deals with the community not only affects the instructional program of his school, but also has a distinct influence upon the entire school district. Lee G. Henderson[6] con-

---

[6] Lee G. Henderson, "A Study of Certain School-Community Relationships with Special Reference to Working Patterns of School Principals" (Unpublished doctoral dissertation, CPFA Project, University of Florida, 1954).

ducted a study of school-community relationships in forty-eight school centers of one large school district. He discovered that the quality of public relations improved as principals increased their use of procedures that involved other people in decision-making. This finding is particularly significant when one realizes that the differences of communities in income and educational level were held constant in his investigation. He also found that community attitudes toward the superintendent, the board of education, and the central staff, as well as toward the local school, were affected by the way principals worked. The principal who uses cooperative procedures wherever practical is following a path that leads to better public relations.

Maintain desirable human relations with the staff. Before an administrator can achieve much in the way of public relations with the community, he needs to be able to create effective working relationships with the staff.[7] Public relations can hardly succeed unless the program is accepted by the school staff as "our program" which "we" helped to build for "our school." Emily M. Scully[8] studied the professional and personal relationships which develop between principals and their teaching personnel as they interact with one another in the course of the daily activities which constitute the life of the school. Through the use of data blanks sent to principals and teachers, she obtained completed returns from sixty-four principals and 1,035 teachers. She discovered that teachers mentioned the principal's personal and professional qualities, his attitudes and modes of behavior as sources of satisfaction and dissatisfaction far more frequently than they mentioned specific aspects of school organization or particular administrative policies or practices. The outstanding professional quality of the principal referred to by over three-fourths of the teachers was his tendency to treat teachers as friends and fellow workers, rather than as subordinates.

The very nature of a successful public relations program is such that the planning of an effective democratic organization is highly necessary. The principal who plans the public relations program in a cooperative manner and who uses the staff wherever possible enhances the possibilities for its success.

---

7 Jones, *op. cit.*, pp. 315–16.
8 Emily M. Scully, "Personnel Administration in Public Education" (Unpublished doctoral dissertation, University of Wisconsin, 1945), p. 315.

Give leadership to the local school.   When the principal's planning and execution of the school's program of public relations are effective, the various activities will give evidence of this efficiency. John F. Locke[9] examined the role of the secondary school principal in public relations and found that three tasks were of primary importance: (1) mobilizing the talents and skills of the staff of a school for a greater mutual understanding and respect for its work; (2) formulating, organizing, and carrying out a program of public relations; and (3) establishing and maintaining ethical and cooperative relationships among the persons involved in the program.

It is the duty of the principal to help familiarize the staff at each level with the general objectives of the over-all program and with the special techniques and procedures applicable at each level. There is a public relations job for every member of the school system to do—a job that is an integral part of his daily work. The school staff, by its very existence and method of functioning, molds the public mind. The principal is responsible for providing leadership that will develop the program and staff to the fullest extent.

The Teacher

The preceding sections have demonstrated that in our highly competitive society both adequate financial support for schools and the economic welfare of teachers depend largely on the good will and support of citizens. Thus, teachers have good reasons for helping to create public understanding of the schools. In the paragraphs that follow some of the more significant ways in which teachers can promote public relations will be reviewed.

Importance of the teacher.   The teacher probably plays the largest and most meaningful role in developing effective public relations for the schools. In the course of his daily work, the teacher comes closer to the home than any other employee in the school. Whether or not the parent ever sees his child's teacher, he hears about the teacher through his child. If a child likes his teacher, he usually likes school, and parents tend to go along with their child's opinion in regard to the teacher. Both in school and out the influence of the teacher is fundamental to a public relations program. If

---

[9] John F. Locke, "Partnership for a Way of Life," *Bulletin of National Association of Secondary School Principals,* XXXII (February, 1948), 52–58.

teachers are enthusiastic about the public relations programs and approve its aims and methods, they are potent forces for direct and effective interpretation.[10]

Classroom vocabulary. Through his vocabulary the teacher can promote or destroy public relations in the classroom. The language that is used and the way in which a thing is told by teachers to pupils affects the reactions of parents to the school. The vocabulary used by the teacher can encourage good public relations if it is appropriate and meaningful to pupils. The manner in which a teacher speaks to the child is important as it affects the way the child will respond. If the teacher often raises his voice unnecessarily when addressing pupils, they are likely to respond in a like manner. Aggressive behavior on the part of the teacher will beget aggressive pupil behavior. The classroom is not an arena for fighting between the teacher and pupil, nor is the teaching situation a contest in which the teacher is pitted against the pupils. The classroom is a place for a cooperative program of work emphasizing meaningful activities of the pupils, with the teacher to lead and to guide the pupils in such activities.

Homework. If properly conceived and carried out, homework may be used by the classroom teacher to advance the cause of public relations. The desire of parents to know about homework is very great. However, opinions and practices with respect to homework vary widely. Some parents think there is too much, some too little; some think it is the wrong kind, and still others are undecided. The simple plan of assign, study, recite is no longer adequate for America's public schools. In today's school the role of the teacher is one of far greater significance than that of a hearer of lessons.

Surveys of present practice show a wide range that begins with no homework and extends to what is termed an excessive amount. Generally, parents approve of homework although individual parents have complained that excessive homework hinders the child's all-round development, arouses rebellion, contributes to careless work habits, and promotes unwholesome attitudes toward the school.[11] Many of the surveys of homework do not give adequate

---

[10] *See* James J. Jones, "The Function of the Teacher in the Public Relations Program," *Georgia Educational Journal,* XLVI (January, 1953), 12.

[11] Lucille G. MaWhinney, "Parents Approve Homework," *Clearing House,* XXIX (April, 1955), 456–58.

detail concerning the kind of homework that is being studied, for the real issue is not the amount but the type of homework that is assigned. If the assigned homework is a mechanical exercise required of all students that is one thing; but if it is a creative project or experiment, or the writing of a research report, that is another thing. If homework is to be meaningful to the pupil, it must be of interest and concern to him. The pupil needs to know what is expected of him at home in terms of preparation, and how this fits into the school picture. Homework assignments that grow naturally out of regular classwork tend to help pupils develop independent study habits and skills. The kind of understanding exemplified by the teacher in giving homework assignments is a big factor in its acceptance by pupils and parents and in promoting public relations. Homework ought to be reasonable in terms of requirements, and should never be used as a punishment.

Discipline. In the guidance of pupil behavior the teacher has an opportunity to help the pupil, to help the learning process, and to promote the understanding of his school. The early concept of discipline that prevailed in this country and took the center of the stage for a while has almost become extinct. In the past little time or effort was expended by the teacher to reconcile teacher demands and pupil abilities. The uniform molds into which children were once forced by teachers' commands have no place in the modern school. Parents still want to be reassured that the school is keeping a reasonably tight rein on behavior, and even parents who may permit excessive freedoms at home are likely to expect control at school. On the other hand, parents may become concerned if school controls are too severe. Only a very limited number of parents favor corporal punishment by the schools.

Teachers and parents alike are concerned about discovering and removing the cause of undesirable behavior in pupils. Disciplinary measures should aim mainly at modifying undesirable social actions; they should not be used merely as punishment for an offense.[12] Teachers need to make certain that disciplinary measures taken by them give redirection to the child, and are not merely devices to relieve their own frustrations. At its peak performance, discipline helps the individual to establish desirable habits of social living. This

---

[12] *See* James J. Jones, "Guidance of Pupil Behavior," *Journal of the National Education Association,* XLIII (March, 1954), 176.

concept envisions taking the pupil from a state of great dependency to a point where he accepts the responsibility for his own behavior. Self-discipline is seen by the teacher as a basis for successful group living, and he uses every opportunity to give pupils a chance to improve their abilities for controlling themselves. Effective discipline is self-discipline whether it is found in school or in life. Teachers who use this approach to guiding pupil behavior tend to promote better public understanding of the work of the school.

Community participation. A teacher will generally accept the fact that the community which provides his means for a livelihood has a right to expect from him at least the participation in community affairs that it expects from members of other professions. The acceptance of this principle by a teacher does not imply that he is to neglect his professional duty in order to be active in community affairs that are completely unrelated to the school and to school work. First, teachers may take an active part in home-and-school associations. Getting to know parents through working with them in an organization that attempts to promote public understanding is highly desirable. Second, teachers may involve the parents in some form of class activity. In many cases, the human resources available to community leaders may have much to offer to special classes in the school. Third, authorities in the field of public relations have found that participation in community activities provides more opportunities for teachers to interpret the school and its program to the community. The final degree of a teacher's success will be determined by his effectiveness in teaching, which in turn is directly conditioned by his knowledge of and acceptance by the community.

Contacts with parents. The classroom teacher has many advantages over the administrator as a public relations person. The frequency and intimacy of the teacher's contacts with parents is often greater than that of the principal or the superintendent. A teacher has more opportunities to meet parents in community group affairs than do his colleagues in the administrative group. The teacher, working through the pupil, of necessity will be in constant contact with many parents and interested patrons. His statements can either win public approval or build resentment in the general public toward his own school and the school system. Teachers ought to have a general understanding of the whole school system and to be able to discuss it intelligently with parents. Likewise, the teacher is in a good position to know what subjects are best not to discuss with parents. One type of information that is considered best to remain in the professional family has to do with a teacher's complaints and concerns about his work, his personal disagreements, and staff personality problems. There is little if any benefit to be derived for the school from discussion of such problems. If parents and citizens ask legitimate questions about the school or school system that go beyond the scope of the teacher's information, he can refer them to the proper source.

Non-instructional Personnel

Non-instructional personnel includes all of those specialized professional and non-professional agents whose work is essential to the facilitation of the instructional process. For the purposes of this discussion, the professional group includes the school physician, dentist, and nurse. The non-professional group includes the secretaries, clerks, and custodians.

Although the teacher remains in the center of the picture for providing a good education, the indirect influence of non-instructional persons and groups of persons has important and crucial effects because of the public images they create for the school. As school services and facilities have expanded, so have the number of people employed to operate and maintain these services and facilities.

It is estimated that there were more than half a million non-teaching people working in the public schools in the United States in 1960.[13] This implies that in the typical school one third of the people on the payroll are not teachers. It is impossible to discuss the public relations possibilities of all the non-instructional personnel in the short space allotted this section. However, the writer has chosen to present data about some of the more significant roles to be played by selected non-teaching persons.

Physicians, dentists, and nurses. The school physician is employed by the local board of education in approximately 25 per cent of the schools in the nation.[14] The typical school physician is a part-time employee who devotes a portion of his time to school medical

---

[13] William H. Roe, *School Business Management* (New York: McGraw-Hill Book Co., Inc., 1961), p. 40.

[14] Delbert Oberteuffer, *School Health Education* (New York: Harper & Row, Publishers, 1954), p. 380.

service. Today, the physician may be said to be a medical-educational consultant to the pupil, as he relates examinations and detection of a pupil's defects to his educational progress.

It is not the purpose of school health services to replace or to reduce the services of private physicians in promoting pupil health. Rather, the school health services are preventive and protective. Pupils are referred to their own private physicians for the correction of revealed defects. A part of the school physician's role is to help parents understand that a school health examination is one of limited scope, and is not to be taken as a substitute for a complete diagnosis. Working with pupils and staff members, the physician is in an excellent position to help interpret the medical and health services of the school to the public.

The school dentist, somewhat like the school physician, begins with an inspection service. Pupils who are discovered to have dental defects are referred to their own private dentists. Emphasis is also placed upon the relationship of nutrition to dental health.

In actual practice, more than half of our schools that are located in cities of more than 2,500 population have some type of school dental program. The larger the city, the more dental health services found in the schools. The trend in America is toward employing more full-time dentists to work for the school districts along with dental hygienists. Through the performance of examinations, referrals, limited treatment, and educational enlightenment, dentists make a great contribution to the school services and to the public relations program of the school or schools in which they practice.

In most modern elementary and secondary schools one can expect to find a well equipped health suite with a school nurse on duty as a part of the school health services. She may be employed by the board of education, the board of health, a voluntary agency, or any combination of these agencies. In the typical situation the school nurse is an employee of the school board and devotes full time to the schools. The position of school nurse is one requiring a high degree of skill in human and public relations as well as technical know-how. Her relationships are rather complex and extend to the administrator, to all members of the school staff, to the pupils, to the parents, and, in some instances, to the community. Through this network of relationships and in the performance of her duties, the nurse is in a strategic position to develop a better understanding of personal and community health and to improve attitudes and health practices. Working through these same relationships, she becomes an important public relations agent for the school.

Secretaries and clerks.   There are few services more essential to the operation of an efficient school system than the secretarial service. These personnel perform services that give balance and tone to the school system. Their work requires skill and tact. As any administrator will admit, he is "quite lost" when an efficient secretary or clerk is absent for only a short time.

The term "secretary" is used most often in a broad sense which includes all types of office workers. To many people a much sharper distinction is in order. Specifically, a "secretary" is a confidential employee of one or more individuals and assumes responsibility for many details and for some minor executive functions. Furthermore, a secretary is a more highly paid employee than a clerk. Generally, the clerk in a school system performs a different assignment than a secretary, but in our present discussion it is inadvisable to make such a sharp distinction; therefore, they will be referred to synonymously as the school secretary or school clerk.

In the course of her work, the school secretary meets many types of persons, including members of the professional staff, members of the non-instructional staff, pupils, parents, and a fairly representative cross section of the general public. She is expected to give and to receive information about various aspects of the school and will hear many complaints and suggestions concerning the work of the school. The role of the secretary is one that calls for her to be a good listener, to make notes of such information as she receives, and to give the data to the proper person.

In an extensive survey of the public relations contacts of school secretaries, the National Education Association collected and analyzed data from 740 secretaries in all types of positions.[15] It found that secretaries generally agree that the impression made by the office, and the attitudes, interests, and appearance of the staff are most important in their public relations contacts. The manner in which a secretary treats people with whom she comes in contact and

---

[15] National Education Association, Research Division, "Public Relations Contacts of Educational Secretaries," Mimeographed (Washington, D.C.: The Association, May, 1956).

the degree of efficiency she maintains are both vital in her total performance as a public relations agent of the school.

School custodians.   The physical appearance of the school building both inside and out creates some type of impression upon visitors to the school. For some citizens this may be their only contact or basis for evaluating education. If the grounds are poorly kept and the interior is untidy, citizens who view these conditions are likely to feel that the educational program is less than first-rate. The cleanliness and orderliness of each school contributes to the health, happiness, and well being of pupils and teachers. Custodians have many contacts at school functions which are attended by the public. The reputation of the school as well as the characters of the custodians are reflected in their manner of dress, in the way they greet the public, and by their general attitudes towards the school. Usually custodians have lived in the community for several years and belong to many organizations. Their work and action reflect the school. This is particularly true in the smaller community where the people see the school through the eyes, ears, and comments of the custodian.[16] With proper training and adequate supervision, custodians can prevent undue depreciation of school property, and can protect it against misuse, vandalism, illegal entry, and damaging activities. They can contribute to the health and safety of school children and create a physical environment conducive to educational efficiency. If they do these things well, they will contribute to the school's public relations program immeasurably.

---

[16] G. A. Rempel, "How the Custodian Operates as a Public Relations Agent," *The Nation's Schools* (September, 1955), p. 96.

CHAPTER V

Techniques of Public Relations

Information for the Public

Education has come to be considered a life-long process; schools are a social device created by the public to provide educational opportunities for youth as a part of this process. Few social institutions, if any, will exist long in a free society without a strong measure of public support. In view of the fact that the schools belong to the public, the people are entitled to be fully informed at all times regarding school problems and needs. What to tell the public and how to choose the media with discretion are important subjects which are worthy of serious consideration.

What to tell the public.   Opinions differ about what to tell the public. Some authorities favor printing all the news while others point out that administrators who do so find themselves in difficulty. Before one can know what or what not to publish, he needs to know the attitudes of specific groups in the community.

One can hardly talk about public relations techniques without calling attention to the weakness of the often made assumption that a direct correlation exists between the flow of information, the absorption of knowledge, and the amount of attitude change. Several years ago Hyman and Sheatsley[1] discovered evidence which indicated (1) that people seek information congenial to the attitudes they already hold; (2) that different people interpret the same information differently; and (3) that information does not necessarily change attitudes. Despite the Hyman-Sheatsley position we continue to rely heavily upon enlarging the flow of information as a solution to many problems. In school public relations inadequate communication is seen as a source of some of our greatest difficulty.

An authority in the area of communications recently stated:

> Campaigns to acquaint the public with issues, public relations
> activities to create a better image, the attempt to saturate the elec-

---

[1] Herbert Hyman and Paul Sheatsley, "Some Reasons Why Information Campaigns Fail," *Public Opinion Quarterly*, XI (1947), 413–23.

torate with their side of the story of political parties during a campaign, are all well known examples of the doctrines of the desirability of an increased flow of information.[2]

The most critical point to be made is that publics, organizations, groups, and individuals all have their own methods and coding systems which select out messages and modify them according to these codes.[3] Perhaps no organization or individual is completely open to all new ideas from its environment.

Yet it can be demonstrated that we accept many common attitudes and beliefs as true without any elaborated ideas or information to support them. W. J. McGuire[4] supports this principle with his many experiments and explanations. He maintains that we accept common attitudes and beliefs without cognitive depth or breadth to bolster them. As the individual often has no differentiated belief structure, when under attack he often lacks the information and arguments with which to reply. One thing that increasing the flow of information to the public may do is to provide more data for information and response.

Truman M. Pierce[5] observed that relatively little conscious effort is being made to keep the rank and file of citizens up to date in matters concerning the increasing functions of education and the possibilities of making schools more effective through the use of new inventions and discoveries in the realm of practice. In order to help meet this need, it is the opinion of the writer that the public ought to be told the facts about the school system and its problems, needs, and successes. In fact, only information which involves possible injury to a teacher's character or which could do personal harm to someone without benefiting the school should be withheld from the public. An example of information that should be withheld is that concerning an employee of the school board who has been accused

[2] Daniel Katz, "Psychological Studies of Communication and Persuasion," in *Communications Research and School-Community Relations* (Cooperative Research Project No. G–037 of the U.S. Office of Education and College of Education, Temple University, Philadelphia, 1956), pp. 58–79.

[3] *Ibid.*, p. 59.

[4] W. J. McGuire, "Resistance to Persuasion Conferred by Active and Passive Prior Refutation of the Same Alternative Counter-Arguments," *Journal of Abnormal and Social Psychology,* LXIII (1961), 326–32.

[5] Truman M. Pierce, *Controllable Community Characteristics Related to the Quality of Education* (New York: Metropolitan School Study Council, Teachers College, Columbia University, 1947).

of some sort of malpractice, although proof is not immediately available. Giving out false information, spreading rumors, or making accusations without definite proof is harmful to the school system.

Choosing media. The effectiveness of school public relations is determined in part by the media selected and the manner in which they are used. Wise selection and use of publicity devices require, in turn, that educators see the relationship between educational interpretation and the basic objective of the public relations program, which is the maintenance of a wholesome two-way relationship between school and community. This objective also implies that appropriate tools must be selected to interpret each element within the entire field of school service. However, one medium seldom will be enough to cover the interpretative needs relating to a given problem or topic. Several media, aptly chosen and developed together, usually will achieve the purpose better than any single device.

Implied in all the functions of the media of mass communication is the obligation to contribute to the education of the members of the community, whether the community is a small village or a large metropolitan area. The schools can develop a basis for proper and intelligent use of the mass media by developing a discriminating and understanding judgment of the products of the mass media. Further, the schools should be aware of the problems as well as the functions of the mass media, so that these can be studied intelligently and better solutions can be found.

Channels of Communication

Considerable research in public relations has been concerned with agencies, avenues or channels, and media for developing understanding between the schools and the public, and with ways of using such means effectively. In fact, the oldest type of research in public relations deals with the various media of communication between the school and its publics. Yet most of these studies are status surveys of such media as state and local school reports, house organs, bulletins, school newspapers, student progress reports, and the public press. It is the purpose of this section of the book to review the most significant and helpful media.

Pupils. Educators regard the pupil as the prime agent in the transmission of information about the school to his parents and home. The character, conduct, and achievements of pupils daily reflect the influence of the school, and would do so in spite of anyone's efforts to the contrary. Laying the foundation for both worthy attainment by its pupils and their good reputation is not only the privilege of the school, but is also its obvious duty. There is little doubt that the loyalty of pupils to an institution that has helped them to get a start in life is contagious. They may pass their appreciation on to others, including adults.

Pupil opportunities in public relations have been recognized by people outside the teaching profession. The following quotation from a congressman bears a message for teachers and school administrators who are concerned with public relations:

> I think it is especially important to reach the school children. I find that going into the schools and talking five or ten minutes to the children, with an opportunity for them to ask questions, gets a bigger play than anything. Every one of those kids goes home and tells his parents. You can make more friends that way than any other way I know.[6]

If an "outsider" or non-educator realizes the value of the school child in the process of public relations, certainly educators can see fit to capitalize upon pupil opportunities.

An experienced administrator is keenly aware of the fact that parental attitudes toward the schools are frequently determined by the sentiments which pupils express around the dinner tables in their homes. He understands that satisfied pupils tend to produce satisfied parents. He knows also that pupils tend to be most vocal about the things they dislike about school. Thus, certain incentives are present to motivate administrators toward using pupils to explain the work of the schools.

The kind of public relations brought about by the pupil-family organization greatly depends upon the school itself. Every student carries home to his parents certain definite impressions of the schools: the type of teacher employed, the fairness or unfairness of teacher and principal, the standard of conduct permitted in the schoolroom, the soundness or futility of the courses studied.

There are many ways in which the pupil can be directly and spe-

---

[6] Roy K. Wilson, "Are Madison Avenue Public Relations Techniques Good Enough for the Schools?" *Bulletin of the National Association of Secondary School Principals,* XLVIII (April, 1964), 79.

cifically drawn into a school public relations program. The most obvious of these would be via the school newspaper. In this situation all the reporting is done by the students. The student thereby becomes the public relations correspondent, relating the story of the school directly through the written word.

Participation in extracurricular activities and in outstanding classroom projects gives the pupil additional opportunities to become a public relations carrier. When the public observes the pupil's participation in such activities the message is almost automatically transmitted. Activities such as art displays, musical programs, and class plays are also among the pupil participation activities which promote public relations.

One area in which students promote good school public relations, and one which many administrators overlook, is the vocational cooperative work experience program. What other function makes such direct contact between school and public? A well organized program, competently directed, with carefully placed students, can certainly promote strong relationships between school, business, and public.

The opportunities for the inclusion of pupils into the public relations program are many and varied. It would, indeed, be wise to capitalize on these as often and effectively as possible.

Parents and parent organizations. The importance of parents and parent organizations in public relations is widely recognized. The best known and the most widely used parent organization is the parent-teacher association, a volunteer organization composed of the parents and teachers of an individual school. The basic purpose of the local association is to improve the efficiency of the school. The local groups usually unite with state groups and with the National Congress of Parents and Teachers.

Most administrators are reluctant to encourage local parent-teacher associations that do not join with the national organization. This reluctance is based upon the fact that local organizations which lose sight of the objectives of the National Congress of Parents and Teachers often tend to think that the primary function of the association is one of raising money. Another cause for complaint comes when a local parent-teacher association attempts to direct the work of the school or to make policy. The basic purpose of the PTA is advisory in nature, whereas the school board, with the advice of its administration, determines policy.

The parent-teacher association has achieved many accomplishments since its inception in 1897 by Alice Birney and Phoebe Hearst. It attempts to give parents an opportunity to discover what their child's teacher is doing for him. The association has conducted outstanding programs of parent education. It has helped school districts in surveys and in securing public opinion on basic issues. The association provides an opportunity for teachers to learn about the parents, homes, and additional data about the children they teach. Much of the research evidence available supports the many possible advantages of the parent-teacher association. It is the duty of the administrator to work closely with the organization and to help clarify its work so that it engages in worthwhile activities. Though the association is an excellent agency through which the partnership concept between the home and school may be effectively established, community organizations in the United States present many variations. Restricting the membership of a community organization to parents establishes certain limits; an overdependence on the PTA may result in inadequate contacts with many citizens whose interest and support are essential.

There are many groups interested in the public schools for various reasons. Some groups want to study and to support the school program; others endeavor to improve the schools or to defend them against unwarranted attacks; and others seek only to find defects. This latter group is composed largely of individuals whose objectives were economy, lower taxes, or censorship, rather than improved education.

A high percentage of the population in many American communities are non-parents, parents whose children have already completed public school, or parents who send their children to private schools because they feel that the public school is not doing the kind of job they wish done. Members of the latter group are often antagonistic toward the public schools. Obviously, a need exists for these people, as well as the parents of public school pupils, to have an understanding of the public school and to communicate their thoughts and ideas to the local school authorities. Some type of lay advice is needed to secure help from this group. A group of persons inside or outside the educational profession, chosen from the school staff or community to advise the school officials, may be known as a "citizens' advisory committee," "lay advisory group," "citizens' council," or "national citizens' commission for public schools," or by a host of similar names. The citizens' group, irrespective of the name assigned to it, can serve as an important means of communication with the public about the school system. Although this body has no legal power to make policy, it can give its advice and recommendations to school officials. It can help collect information and data with regard to public opinion about school concerns, and thus can help prevent the school administrators from being overcome with data from a vocal minority. Citizen advisory groups are desirable and can do much to aid public relations. Perhaps their greatest benefit lies in the bringing together of many non-parents and parents whose children have already completed their stay in the local schools. They help to give the administrator a viewpoint of citizens other than parents.

Community groups. There are organizations to be found in every community capable of rendering some service in the development of a school-community relations program. In the smaller community many of these groups possess proportionately greater influence than their fellow organizations in larger centers, where greater diversity and competition of outside interests tend to restrict the orbit of power of a single unit. Moehlman and Van Zwoll[7] list and describe the following organizations in terms of their interests, value, and means: (1) civic, (2) cultural, (3) economic, (4) political, (5) professional, (6) social, (7) women's groups, and (8) welfare groups. Despite the fact that these groups are not as closely related to school activities as are the parent and parental groups, it is essential for the school to study each type of organization with the thought of finding some helpful way in which to interest the group in public education.

Most of these organizations are national in scope and the local pattern of organization and function is well standardized. Since the type of the organization conditions both its program and membership, it is necessary for the schools to study each category in terms of the nature of the material and the possibilities for the development of specific programs.

---

[7] Arthur B. Moehlman and James A. Van Zwoll, *School Public Relations* (New York: Appleton-Century-Crofts, Inc., 1957), pp. 416–26.

Definitive research concerning service clubs is almost nonexistent in the literature. However, Lloyd F. Rumbaugh[8] has attempted to identify, classify, and analyze the educational activities of the major service clubs—the Rotary International, the Lions International, and the Kiwanis International—for a one-year period. Data were secured from the local service clubs' activities reports on file in the home offices of each club, and from a random sampling of 300 clubs from each federation. The major service clubs have been actively engaged in providing clothing, aid, support, parties, recreational facilities, and in some cases, camps for America's needy youth. Of course, their personal contacts and public relations contributions extend beyond the activities described here.

School reports and publications. The annual report of the superintendent is very near the oldest and certainly is one of the best means of telling the public what the schools are attempting to do. Yet many reports still fail to interest the average reader because they are mechanical records of certain facts relating to the formal operation of the school system, and give little evidence of having been prepared for public relations purposes. Any school executive who does not publish an annual report that is meaningful to the public is failing to make use of one of the best public relations techniques available to administrators. The system-wide report offers opportunity for the creative superintendent to tell the school story with pictures, data, and words that will help citizens and parents understand how their money is being spent and what the schools are doing.

Pupil progress reports. The pupil progress report is used to inform the parent and the pupil about his progress in school. Parents are often dissatisfied with reports that tell little about their child, and it is the responsibility of the school to prepare and distribute reports to parents that are meaningful and useful. Each of the many forms of reports to the parent has its own advantage, and no single report is best for all schools.

Although the objections to the traditional report card are well known, many of the public schools continue to use it. One method used to supplement the traditional card is the narrative report. Where teachers have sufficient skills to use this form properly, it is

---

[8] Lloyd F. Rumbaugh, "The Educational Activities of the Major Service Clubs," *University of Pittsburgh Bulletin*, XL, No. 3 (1944), 227–35.

an excellent method for describing individual differences and academic achievements of the pupil. Parent-teacher conferences can be a very effective method of reporting pupil progress. Some schools using more than one method of reporting find the combination advantageous. An insightful and creative teacher can think of additional ways to use reports to promote understanding and to create good will toward the school.

Other types of reports and publications often sent to the home of pupils include school bulletins, school newspapers, school newsletters, parent handbooks, and special reports. The purpose of special reports and publications is to provide the public with timely data about a single subject or a particular phase of the school program that may need immediate attention. They supplement the regularly published reports, and will vary from time to time and from school to school, depending upon the needs and conditions that prevail.

Personal contacts. Authorities in public relations stress the importance of personal contacts between school personnel and the public. Home visitation by members of the staff can be an excellent device for promoting public relations if it is used in a wholesome manner. In large urban areas it may be possible to train specialists for this work, but in smaller school systems it may be necessary to use home-room teachers. If regular teachers are used for home visits, caution must be exercised so as to use only those teachers who are capable of sympathetic understanding of home conditions, who can devote sufficient time to the activity, and who are interested in it. The planning ought to be made in a manner that encourages initial invitations to come freely from the home. In most instances teachers should not go into homes where they have not been invited. People who represent the school should make prior arrangements before making a home visit. Teachers who are expected to make home visits need to have their work load reduced somewhat, as this type of activity is time-consuming. All efforts by the teacher should be directed toward a better understanding of the home and the pupil.

Perhaps the most extensively used personal contact procedure is the urging of parents to visit the school during regular school sessions. One of the ultimate purposes of having parents visit the school is to get them where records and other materials concerning their sons and daughters are immediately available. One such successful practice is reported in which the school invites five parents to visit the school each day.[9] The purposes of the parent visits are: (1) to familiarize parents with the personnel, plant, curriculum, and activities available; (2) to provide teachers with opportunities for discussing student problems with them; (3) to give students a chance to acquaint parents with the school environment; (4) to help parents get information about school problems; (5) to encourage parents to regard school visits as a part of their normal activity; and (6) to educate students to the fact that parents should take an active part in planning school activities. In this program parents are chosen from an alphabetical list and five are invited daily to arrive at school by 10 A.M. and to stay as long as they desire. They are given a copy of their child's schedule and may either visit with him or inspect any part of the school program they desire. Visitors are encouraged to eat in the lunchroom and to cover the entire campus. Before departing, parents are requested to visit with the principal and to discuss any part of the school program they observed. The principal may ask them for their evaluation.

The type of school visitation described here has many benefits in promoting public relations. First, it gets away from the idea that parents are only expected to visit during Education Week. Second, it permits freedom in visiting classrooms and indicates that there is nothing to hide from school patrons. Third, it provides an opportunity that many parents want but may never request. Fourth, this plan was conducted at a high school where parents usually do not visit their children as often as they do in the elementary grades.

Another method of personal contact often used by school personnel is the telephone call. Such contact may be used to secure information about the pupil or his health, to arrange for a conference with the parent, to invite the parent to visit the school, to ask the parent to accept a school responsibility, or to talk about a mutual school problem. In this form of personal contact, one would do well to avoid long discussions where tempers flare about serious problems. Although the telephone provides a quick service for thanking someone who has been of help to you with school activities and problems, it is always well to use the telephone for the purposes listed above and to arrange for the parent to come for a conference where a face-to-face relationship can be established. Through the use of intimate personal relations the small community affords the

---

[9] James J. Jones, "Three Technics for Bettering School-Community Relations," *The Nation's Schools,* LV (April, 1955), 82.

school personnel an opportunity to develop an understanding of the school and to discover community needs as well.

Special events.   Another excellent source for developing better public understanding of the work of the school and the school system is the activities of the school to which the public is invited. If one were to single out the source which affords more contact with people than any other, it probably would be these activities. There are several basic reasons why this is true. First and foremost, parents and grandparents enjoy seeing their children and grandchildren perform and act. Even though the part assigned to a child may be small and simple, parents and relatives will go to the school to see the performance. Second, the students themselves feel the need for social and recreational activities. Many of the school activities to which the public is invited are referred to by various names, such as "cocurricular," "extraclass," "out-of-class," "allied," and "student" activities. As used here, activities refers to those functions which are initiated and supervised by the school, are eminently educational in nature, and are an integral part of the school program. Studies indicate that the values which have been attributed to extracurricular activities are regarded as pertinent to a program of general education.

These student activities are numerous and varied, and are increasing in number and significance all the time. Among the type of activities included are contests of various kinds, such as debates and athletics; programs in celebration of special days and events, such as Columbus Day, Washington's Birthday, Lincoln's Birthday, Thanksgiving, and Christmas. Other special events give recognition to the dedication of a new school plant, school exhibits, bazaars, festivals, and fairs. Additional events to which the public is invited are special visiting days, school plays, musical programs, recreational nights, and the array of events associated with commencement. No attempt is made here to list all the special events to which the public may be given an invitation. Any activity that is sponsored by the school in which an opportunity is provided for the public to participate or serve as an audience is an effective medium for public relations. When parents visit the schools and see for themselves some of the activities in which their children take part, they can hardly escape being somewhat conditioned in a favorable manner toward the school.

Newspapers.   A large number of content analyses of public newspapers has shown that athletics and extraclass activities are topics of news given more space in the press than any other aspect of the schools' functions. Yet there is much evidence to indicate that although the subject of extracurricular affairs is highest in amounts of newspaper space, it is lowest in terms of parent interest. One possible explanation for this disproportion between coverage and interest is based upon the fact that the basic purpose of the newspaper is to publish information and news. Newspapers give publicity to school news and donate literally thousands of dollars worth of space free of charge; in addition, they often contribute free advertising of forthcoming events which are money-making in nature and for which they would ordinarily charge most other organizations. On the other hand, the treatment of school news by the newspapers should not in any sense be thought of as charity to the schools. Publishing school news is a business proposition for the newspaper as it deliberately includes school news with the hope that this will help circulation.

As a channel of communication, the newspaper must be given a high rating because so many people read the newspaper and probably receive as much, if not more, information from it than from any other single source. Almost everyone reads at least one or more newspapers daily. Along with providing information, the newspaper expresses opinion through its editorials. These opinions influence the thoughts and actions of its readers.

The newspaper provides a rare opportunity for administrators and school people to make use of this unusual agency to provide the public with information about schools. Administrators will need to seize the initiative and demonstrate to newspaper editors their willingness to cooperate. The press and the school personnel need to reach a mutual understanding about working arrangements which implement a news policy. Perhaps the superintendent and the director of public relations need to confer with editors of all papers serving the school district and to develop working agreements mutually acceptable to both groups concerning the newspaper as a medium of public relations. Working together, the newspaper and the school have tremendous responsibilities in their power to influence the thinking of people in a given area.

Radio. The American people spend many hours a week listening to radio broadcasts. In fact, over 98 per cent of the homes in this country have at least one radio. In the typical home at least one person listens to radio two hours or more daily. This home listening is supplemented by the use of several million other radios in automobiles and in public places. Thus the radio provides a wide listening audience for telling the school story.

The basic ideas of mutual understanding and cooperative planning for effective working relationship experience in regard to newspaper editors also apply to school-radio relationships. Most broadcasters feel a sense of public responsibility. The commercial functions of a broadcasting station have to meet the requirements of what the Federal Communications Act of 1934 calls the "public interests." Generally, stations allocate 25 per cent or more of broadcasting time for free "public service" announcements and programs. These broadcasts are intended to be nonpartisan and to inform the public about public issues and problems. Schools usually get a very reasonable portion of this broadcast time. Of course, the station manager has the right to decide if school suggestions for programs are appropriate.

Many large school systems own their broadcasting stations and provide regular programs for pupils and the community. Small school systems often arrange with a neighboring commercial station for free periodic broadcasts. Schools can aid greatly by taping, in accordance with station standards, many school events which are useful for radio broadcasts. The radio has much to contribute in helping the public to understand the problems and needs of the schools.

Television.   Although television is much younger than radio and much more costly, it is experiencing rapid growth in this country. More than 80 per cent of American homes have at least one television set. In the typical home television is viewed by one or more persons for approximately six hours during the day and evening. Television has the capacity to bring people and programs into our living rooms. One may see the performer in action, hear his skillful use of speech, and watch his gestures with rapt attention.

Most of the working relationships discussed with regard to newspaper editors and radio station managers apply to television. Planning with station managers and developing working agreements concerning program proposals are a must if administrators and school people wish to derive maximum benefit from this medium for public relations. School personnel should have program proposals ready to submit to station managers when asking for broadcast time, as busy station staff members have their own work schedules to perform. In planning, it is important to have each broadcast serve a particular purpose or function.

The potentials of television for classroom instruction are not fully known at this time. However, the use and significance of television on public relations are much greater than those of radio. The addition of sight to sound makes the program more personal and direct. As a medium of communications, television has almost unlimited potential.

Other Contacts

A survey by Delmas F. Miller revealed more than 800 activities considered to be a part of the public relations program.[10] Therefore, no effort can be expended here to present all the channels of communications or techniques of public relations available or used in present practice. In addition to those channels of communication already treated in this chapter, two other contacts are presented.

Successful teaching. Although this topic has been touched upon in Chapter IV, it is one deemed worthy of further comment. It is in the classroom, on the playground of the school, and in the community that the most lasting and most vital public relations attitudes are built. There is no doubt that today's schools are building their public relations for tomorrow. It is during the formative years of childhood and youth that permanent regard for education and for the benefits that may be gained by remaining in school until graduation is formed. If the child, or youth, has met with hostility, frustration, and bitterness through inadequate curriculums and teaching personnel insensitive to the needs of the pupils—as is sometimes the case— nothing will help the schools. People who have dropped out of school because they felt that the curriculums were not meeting their needs, or that teachers had not given consideration to the attitudes, interests, or abilities that they possessed would hardly be friendly toward voting more money for the support of public education. Schools should be staffed by the ablest teachers obtainable. Teachers

---

[10] Delmas F. Miller, "An Appraisal Technique for Programs of Public School Relations" (Unpublished doctoral dissertation, University of Pittsburgh, 1943).

who are proud of their profession, convinced of their importance to society, well trained to do their job, and who understand the importance of developing attitudes and habits along with skills in subject matter are one of the most potent forces for public relations.

Mutual understanding.   The concept of mutual understanding implies that communication involves a two-way process. There must be an understanding of the community by the school and an understanding of the school and its work by the community. Although the school is but one of many social agencies that works for the child, it represents the place where children spend most of their waking hours. The school needs to share its information about the child with the community, and vice versa. One of the best ways to improve learning opportunities for children is through the whole-hearted cooperation of school and community. Wise administrative leadership will tend to promote this goal.

Finally, it should be emphasized again that any program of public relations, even when cooperatively arrived at and implemented, is the prime responsibility of the administrative portion of the schools. Responsibility for the amount and type of information which is made known to the public concerning the school program is an administrative function. Ways of involving all of the public in the community in planning the school program and carrying out the plans are also the concern of the administrative officials.

CHAPTER VI

The School Plant

The term "school plant" includes the site, the buildings, and the equipment necessary to operate a school. To a large extent any institution is interpreted through visual symbols such as its plant and facilities. Because of the concreteness and tangibility of the school plant, this physical plant represents the space interpretations of the educational program of the public schools. It can be seen, felt, and used. Unlike public funds expended for personnel, moneys spent for plant and facilities are visible and meaningful to the general public even when school is not in session. These are relatively permanent possessions of the school system and are constructed to be used for many years.

Public relations are involved in fulfilling the purpose of the school plant and in planning, operating, maintaining, and using the facilities. How well the administrator plans for and carries out these functions will determine to a high degree how successful the public relations program will be.

Purpose of the School Plant

The primary purpose of the school plant is to facilitate the instructional program. It is expected to house the pupils and the staff and to expedite the attainment of a desirable educational program. The best possible educational environment should be planned around and for the children. It must care for their psychological and physical needs. The building must be safe, healthful, comfortable, and inviting. The school building is the child's home away from home since he is likely to spend the greater part of his waking hours in school. The whole school plant must be such that the energy applied to the learning process itself may be expended with a minimum of waste. Every activity to be carried on in a school ought to be thoroughly considered in the planning of that particular school building. Since activities are subject to change, the facility should be sufficiently flexible to be adapted readily and economically to changing needs.

In several instances the organizational structure of the school system has been greatly influenced by the available school buildings. For example, the junior high school has increased in popularity in many American communities as it has served to relieve overcrowding in both the elementary and senior high schools. Of course, this type of short term planning and hasty action is based upon the convenience of buildings rather than upon sound educational goals and purposes. In the long run this type of short-term planning has a tendency to do a grave injustice to the junior high school program. The school plant is one of the most necessary and important agencies in a program of public relations. It is a storehouse of opportunity for interpreting the school program to the public.

Planning School Facilities

Personnel involved. If the school plant is to promote the understanding of the school and its activities, it is virtually essential that many people be involved in its planning. Although widespread participation in planning offers no guarantee that the plans will be accepted, it does provide an opportunity for the public to know what is involved in such action and to make suggestions. The general public is entitled to have information on local school plant needs and proposed school plant programs. One of the best sources of public information on school plant needs is a well planned, long range school plant program.

As the chief executive officer of the board, the superintendent of schools has the responsibility for school plant planning. It does not automatically follow that he will do the actual work, either alone or with help from the administrative staff. Deciding the nature of participation and who shall participate may be based upon: (1) the extent and complexity of the study; (2) the advisability of postponing or leaving undone certain other work; (3) the ability of the superintendent and his staff to handle the technical aspects of the study; and (4) the need for an independent check on local thinking.[1] If the administrative staff does possess enough specialists in research and school plant problems, the study may be conducted with little

---

[1] John E. Herrick, *et al., From School Program to School Plant* (New York: Henry Holt and Company, 1956), p. 133.

or no outside help. Most authorities concerned with school plants and public relations suggest that, even under these conditions, professional and non-professional employees, citizens of the community, and possibly pupils be used in some manner.

Another type of approach involves the cooperative study, in which committees of teachers or other school personnel and groups of lay citizens are to be involved in the study of local building problems. If this type of approach is used, the superintendent and the board of education must be fully convinced of its significance and be prepared to exercise patience and understanding with all committee work, reports, and recommendations. If proper planning, orientation, and coordination are not carried out, more harm than good may be an outcome of this type of approach.

Much of the controversy concerning who ought to take part in the planning of school facilities centers around the use of lay citizens. The weight of the evidence tends to favor participation of citizens along with professional, consultants, and other school employees. Admitting that laymen generally know little about school buildings, it is believed that providing them with opportunity to take part in planning buildings may improve their understanding about school construction problems. Where long range planning is practiced by the administrator, citizens participation delays planning only little, if at all. The use of lay citizens to help plan school facilities provides them with opportunities to learn about school building costs and related problems. According to N. E. Viles,[2] it is sometimes necessary, even with a well planned public relations program, for those in charge to provide specific information on needs and costs when construction funds are to be voted and at various other times during the program.

Planning procedures. The type of school building required in a particular community is tied to the type of educational experiences needed for the children in the educational program. The basic steps to be followed in planning a new plant can be outlined as follows:

> 1. Analyze the educational needs of the community and determine the future school program as a basis for the evaluation of existing facilities as well as for the planning of new or remodeled ones.
> 2. Survey the entire school district to establish a master plan

---

[2] N. E. Viles, *Local School Construction* (Washington, D.C.: U.S. Department of Health, Education, and Welfare, 1957), p. 9.

which should give consideration to the possibility of district reorganization where this is likely to occur.

3. Select and acquire any sites needed to implement the over-all approved plan resulting from the survey.

4. Develop the educational specifications for each separate project in the approved master plan.

5. Design each separate project in accordance with the approved educational specifications.

6. Secure bids, let contracts, and erect the buildings in accordance with the approved working drawing.

7. Equip the completed building and put it into use.[3]

The beginning step in planning a school building is to discover the educational needs and to compare them with existing facilities in order to decide what additional buildings will be needed. The manner in which the administrator deals with the public and the way in which he capitalizes upon the opportunities for public relations may depend upon his knowledge of public relation techniques. Almost every step listed in the planning procedure offers suitable opportunities for enhancing public relations.

The dedication. A competent school administrator seldom forgets that the schools belong to the people. Consequently, he exercises tremendous effort to continuously inform the public through a program of sound interpretation. Such an administrator recognizes the opportunities for public relations that surround the opening of a new school plant. He will use newspaper articles, formal dedication ceremonies, and open house programs to tell the school story. Perhaps the dedication ceremony will be the only formal orientation for the general public. At the dedication of a school plant the program is devoted to a general overview of the events leading to the need for the building and the relationship of the educational program to the construction of the building. Special features of the building may be emphasized and the program itself supplemented through the use of colored slides or film with comments or speakers.

The purposes of these activities are: (1) to explain the building; (2) to explain the school program; (3) to solicit interest and cooperation of the public; and (4) to thank all who helped with the planning, including the general public.[4]

---

[3] National Council on Schoolhouse Construction, *Guide for Planning School Plants* (Nashville, Tenn.: The Council, 1958), p. 1.

[4] Herrick, *op. cit.,* pp. 215–17.

Although the public may be told about the building through several media, it is always desirable to get the public to see the new building first-hand. An open house or dedication program, which may include a tour of the plant with staff and pupils serving as guides, should be held when the largest number of citizens can attend. Printed brochures which include floor plans are helpful to the tourists. Special personnel can be placed at strategic points to explain the unusual features of the plant. Also, displays, posters, and selected teachers may be used to interpret the school program. Factory representatives may be present to demonstrate any of their equipment that has been installed in the building. To inspire continued interest and support of the school system, it is customary to have a well known speaker give a formal address in which he gives facts about long range plans, the current program, and problems to be faced in the future. It is also customary to thank all the people who have made the construction of the building possible.

Citizens who are unable to attend the dedication ceremony can be given the opportunity to visit the plant at another time. Again, they must be shown every courtesy and provided the written materials available about the plant.

Trends in school building. In the field of school building construction we are witnessing some of the greatest changes in the entire area of education. Comparing a modern school plant with one constructed twenty years ago brings out startling innovations. One change in direction is toward more creativity in design and construction. Most of these changes have been made as a result of study and creativity on the part of architects and the tremendous amount of time and study given to the cause by the superintendents, consultants, and board members. The following trends are the most discernible:

1. Planning of the school building from the "inside-out."
2. Greater participation in the planning process.
3. The greater use of specialized resource persons in the planning process.
4. Increased size and uniqueness of the design of instructional spaces.
5. Increased concern with flexibility in design.
6. More concern for the shape and form of the building.
7. Larger sites.

8. A conception of the building as something more than a collection of classrooms.

9. More consideration to the quality as well as the quantity of lighting.

10. Greater importance of the thermal environment.

11. Increasing variety of materials and techniques of construction.

12. Concern for aesthetics.[5]

Of the twelve trends listed above, the second, greater participation or cooperative planning, is the key to better public relations in regard to school plants. The trend toward close cooperation between the architect, board of education, administration, faculty, school employees, and lay citizens is increasing. It is no longer considered sufficient for the superintendent and the board of education to be the sole judges of the architect's plans and specifications.[6] The concept of using the best thinking of all concerned through a cooperative process will improve school plant planning and public relations.

Operation of the School Plant

The management of school plants involves all of the services, activities, and procedures concerned with keeping existing school facilities open and in usable condition. "Operation of plant," a phase of plant management, may be defined "as those activities which are concerned with keeping the physical plant open and ready for use," and includes cleaning, disinfecting, heating, moving furniture, caring for grounds, and other related housekeeping chores.[7] Operation of the plant has a distinct place in the school budget and should not be confused with maintenance of school plant which will be discussed later. Only in small school systems will operation and maintenance of school plant be considered as one function. Keeping the school plant open and ready for use demands the services of custodial personnel and the provision of proper custodial supplies. For

---

[5] Stephen J. Knezevich, *Administration of Public Education* (New York: Harper & Row, Publishers, 1962), pp. 475–78.

[6] Emery Stoops and M. L. Rafferty, Jr., *Practices and Trends in School Administration* (New York: Ginn and Company, 1961), p. 241.

[7] Paul L. Reason, Emery M. Foster, and Robert F. Will, *The Common Core of State Educational Information* (Washington, D.C.: U.S. Office of Education, 1953), p. 8.

these purposes the typical school system annually spends approximately 8–9 per cent of its current funds.

Operational plant needs. Formerly, custodial services for schools were primarily concerned with cleaning the floors, dusting the furniture, firing furnaces, and similar duties. The work was poorly organized and the results were left to chance. Custodians were not considered very important people; they were paid low wages and had meager equipment with which to work. At that time public relations was not one of their considerations.

Today, these practices are not so prevalent as they were formerly. Growing emphasis upon adequate school facilities, combined with better knowledge about the learning environment, health, and safety, as well as the use of school facilities by the general public, have encouraged boards of education and administrators to comprehend the value of adequate custodial services and the significance of providing trained people to provide them. This trend is best described in a quotation on general administration by Stoops and Rafferty:

> As more of modern science enters into the maintenance and operation of a school plant, the position of custodian will be revolutionized. Instead of a broken-down elderly man, as in too many places he has been, the custodian will become an educated, scientifically trained, and well-paid professional. The trend is in the direction of more careful screening and in-service training of custodial and maintenance employees.[8]

Scientific methods are becoming as essential in the operation of a school plant as in any other administrative activity. New methods of carrying out housekeeping chores are calling for more research in terms of time and motion studies, cost analyses, and objective job appraisals.

Purposes of custodial service. Accompanying the newly defined operational school plant needs are certain well defined purposes of custodial service. Among these purposes are: (1) preserving property values; (2) protecting health and safety; (3) providing a climate for learning; (4) developing good will; (5) maintaining cleanliness and neatness; and (6) effecting operating economies.[9]

---

[8] Stoops and Rafferty, *op. cit.*, p. 272.

[9] R. N. Finchum, *School Plant Management: Administering the Custodial Program* (Washington, D.C.: U.S. Department of Health, Education, and Welfare, 1961), p. 2.

When one considers the far-reaching effects of any of these purposes, it becomes immediately apparent that the custodial service is the key factor in the operation of the school plant. Although a brief mention is made of the custodian in Chapter IV under the heading of "Non-instructional Personnel," a more detailed description of his relationships within the school system and with the general public follows.

Relations with the public. A school custodian can be one of the most important public relations forces in the school. This potentially valuable service must be brought to his attention, and in-service training must be developed to help him grow and to improve his efficiency in this area. His daily actions make a strong impression upon children and adults alike—especially upon those in his building and upon those with whom he comes in daily contact.

In addition to being an essential tool in the educational process, the school plant plays a significant part in public relations. Despite many criticisms to the contrary, the public school is one of the most important social institutions in a community. Many favorable aspects of the school plant may be developed through efficient management of the custodial service. Often the children's impressions of the school building, as well as those of many adults who visit or see it in passing, are established by the type of custodial services that keep the building clean, attractive, and comfortable. For some children it may be the cleanest and nicest home they have witnessed.

Some parents will be likely to judge the school by the way in which the custodian performs his duties and the manner in which he conducts himself at public functions held at the school. For two main reasons, the custodial staff should be employed on a twelve months' basis where this is feasible. First, employment of the custodian throughout the year results in the obtaining of a better qualified type of employee. Second, someone is responsible for the care and protection of the school buildings, equipment, and grounds during the summer months. Again, this additional employment gives more public relations advantages to service personnel.

Members of the custodial staff must be able to work cooperatively with other employees within the school system. They have to exercise the same discretion that professional employees do in discussing school affairs and activities. Part of the in-service education program should be devoted to helping the custodial staff understand the purposes of education in order that they may perform their duties better and be of more help with school functions. If custodians recognize their role in public relations and receive help and encouragement, they can make a strong contribution to the public relations program.

Maintenance of the School Plant

Although maintenance is often confused with operation of the school plant, in terms of definition and budgetary procedures they are quite different. In terms of financial accounting, "maintenance" refers to keeping the school site, the building, and the equipment in as near their original state of repair as possible. There is a close correlation between the quality of custodial service and the need for building maintenance. A working definition for maintenance would entail repairs and replacements, although most maintenance charges are for repairs. Generally, the typical school district spends 4–5 per cent of its current budget in the area known as school plant maintenance.

Purposes of maintenance.   The over-all purpose of maintenance is similar to that of operation—that is, keeping the school facilities in such condition that they will meet the needs of the educational program. Specific purposes of maintenance may be defined as those activities and services which help: (1) promote health and safety; (2) provide operating economies; (3) prevent time loss; (4) preserve property values; (5) retard deterioration; (6) prevent obsolescence; and (7) develop community pride.[10] These purposes serve as guidelines to procedures for carrying on an effective program of school plant maintenance.

Importance of maintenance.   As soon as the school board formally accepts a new school building, obsolescence begins. At this point the construction is completed and the life of the building is generally dependent upon how it is operated and maintained. School buildings are the largest pieces of equipment that a community or a school district is likely to own, and the necessity for obtaining optimum services from them, as well as for protecting the district's finan-

---

[10] R. N. Finchum, *School Plant Management: Organizing the Maintenance Program* (Washington, D.C.: U.S. Department of Health, Education, and Welfare, 1960), pp. 7–15.

cial investment, results in the efforts expended upon maintaining the facilities in a high state of repair. Although it seems self-evident that expenditures for maintenance will accomplish these purposes, this has not always been the case. Expenditures of this type make it possible to have a cleaner, healthier, safer school environment, and buy additional years of usefulness, thus prolonging the dates for replacing various parts of school facilities. Many school boards think that, if the budget has to be reduced, plant maintenance is something that can be postponed and that school will keep for the next year. The falsity in this type of thinking lies in the fact that future maintenance may be much more expensive and replacements may be called for much earlier than they would have been under normal conditions.

The public school plant, usually planned and often financed through cooperative community efforts, frequently represents the most substantial as well as the most important community investment.[11] Since the plant is dedicated to school and community uses and represents a major community interest, it should be so maintained that it merits continued community appreciation and strong financial support. Effective school plant management programs demand diligent planning; they do not just happen. A well kept plant should be a source of pride and joy to the people who use it as well as to those who view and help pay for it. The public has learned to accept clean and well kept buildings as a criterion for judging the merits of the entire school program. Therefore, when patrons observe a well kept school plant, they are most likely to conclude that their children are in good hands.

Beautification of the interior. To beautify the foyers, corridors, special rooms, and all types of classrooms through such means as proper color treatment, mural paintings, beautiful pictures, and growing plants, is to fulfill a need for upkeep that affects everyone who uses a building. In far too many school plants little attention is given these matters. The challenge of making the school environment more beautiful offers an opportunity to create more interest in the school by the public. When one really considers the significance of beauty to a school building and the ease of securing it, it is very difficult to comprehend why some school officials and employees neglect this matter. The cost is not prohibitive, as one color of paint

---

[11] *Ibid.,* p. 2.

does not cost more than another. Mural painting may be included as part of the original capital outlay used to purchase the site and plant. Lovely pictures may be purchased or they may be painted by the students of art. Another method of financing beautification projects is to encourage the graduating class to present a picture, a painting, or some other type of art to the school as a class remembrance. Some communities obtain funds for such needs through shows, athletic contests, art exhibits, and donations from interested citizens. In the final analysis, it is not the cost that prohibits beautification in many instances, but the lack of understanding of the need for beauty and its effect upon all who come in contact with it. Public relations demands that beauty accompany the school plant.

Beautification of exterior and grounds.   The exterior of the school plant and the grounds that surround it are important parts of beautification that cannot be ignored. A school ground planting scheme will generally consist of seeded lawns, foundation plantings to "tie" the buildings to the ground, intersection planting of hardy shrubs at angles and curves of drives and walks, tall trees to frame the building, and trees planted in groves for shade.[12] Through the use of trees, shrubbery, flowers, grass, proper grading of the site, and other landscaping effects, an unsightly building may be changed into an attractive plant. Boards of education in financially restricted districts often omit landscaping the grounds. Having provided a place for people to meet, they fail to see the real value and importance of beautification of the outside of the building to all who may view it. Even in a school district where finance is limited, the school employees may use Arbor Day to add trees, shrubbery, flowers, grass, and other acts of beautification. In most states, the state university has a school of agriculture that will provide many helpful free suggestions on landscaping. Likewise, the state departments of education often publish manuals containing useful suggestions for improving and beautifying school grounds.

Once the school grounds have been made attractive they must be kept that way through proper care and upkeep. A planned program of upkeep is necessary, and the cooperation of the faculty and pupils should be secured in protecting the plants and in keeping the school grounds relatively free of litter. Pupils can be taught to re-

---

[12] American Association of School Administrators, *American School Buildings* (Washington, D.C.: The Association, 1949), p. 78.

spect and care for their school building through developing a sense of pride in their own campus. When the school site and the school plant are thoughtfully planned as a unit, much of the site will function as a logical extension of the building itself. This blending of building and site makes a pleasing appearance for those who come into daily contact with the campus. There are times when site beautification must be subordinated to recreational use, but the grass, flowers, shrubs, and trees will serve as a source of enjoyment for the pupils and will help them remember school as a pleasant experience.

Other School Plant Related Activities

Telephone conversations. Most telephone calls in public schools are made by school administrators, teachers, secretaries, and clerks as a part of their daily work. Likewise, calls are received by these persons. In order for the general public to have access to telephone numbers of the school, the numbers are listed in the yellow pages of the telephone directory. These listings are often supplemented by school publications which carry the school telephone number and are sent to the homes of pupils. After being able to secure the correct telephone number, the public want to be able to get through the switchboard and to reach the party they are calling without undue waiting or having to re-dial. Often what is needed is additional switchboards with a sufficient number of lines to handle the telephone calls that are being made. The telephone companies are happy to make a study of each local school and to advise the administration about their telephone needs.

One of the perplexing problems in telephone usage concerning staff members other than office personnel who make and receive calls in the school office, can be handled rather simply. This type of interruption can be eliminated by the installation of an adequate number of telephones located at strategic places throughout each building.

Having ample telephones installed is no positive proof that they will be used in an efficient manner to promote better communication and good will. In receiving calls, the person who answers should give the name of his school or the administrator's office and his own name. The caller should be referred to the appropriate person as soon as possible. Telephones should certainly be answered promptly and messages taken correctly.

The telephone conversation ought to be carried on in a normal tone of voice. When answering long distance calls, secretaries and others should make sure the connection is clear before having the administrator attempt to engage in conversation that may not be heard. Where problems exist in hearing or speaking on the telephone, it may be necessary to ask the telephone company to give suggestions or help. The telephone is one of the most common contacts between the public school and the public. How the calls are handled has a lasting effect upon public relations and what the public thinks about the schools.

Correspondence. To hold a responsible position, whether in business, public education, or industry, or to succeed in most professions, one needs to know how to communicate effectively by letter. The school administrator, teacher, or other school employee who knows how to communicate by the use of a letter is in position to make new friends and to create good will. Letters of complaint may have to be written, as mistakes happen in the best of organizations. The purpose of such a letter is not to "let off steam," but to get the mistake corrected as promptly as possible. One should remember that the person receiving the letter is not always the one responsible for the error. Letters of request or inquiry may also have to be written. They should be brief and should simply provide a statement or two telling what is desired. If one is requesting information, he should begin by explaining briefly his reason for writing, and then go directly to his questions. Writing letters of application may sometimes be a part of one's job. In a very large sense, a letter of application is a sales letter; the letter writer is trying to sell himself or to convince a prospective employer that he is the right person for a particular job. The appearance of the letter, its tone, organization, grammer, sentence structure, spelling, and punctuation all tell something about one's ability and training. No doubt there will be many other types of correspondence that will involve the school and school system. All letters that are sent from the school should be warm and friendly and should possess an orderly content that tends to elicit a positive response from its recipient. Form letters are to be avoided wherever possible, but when they are to be used, they should be given the same careful attention that other letters receive, including the use of letterhead stationery, high quality paper, and careful typing. The recipient of a letter from a school or school system tends to evaluate the school in terms of the type correspondence he has received.

Parent conferences. The purpose of any parent conference, whether planned or informal, is to promote better understanding between the teacher and the parent so that the child may benefit. This kind of getting together helps the parent gain a more complete understanding of his child's ability, work habits, and adjustment to school. It also enables the teacher to tell the school story and particular incidents about the child that would not ordinarily be sent home through reports. Parent conferences enable the parent to see samples of his child's work and to see the best work the child is capable of doing.

Since most parent conferences take place in the school building—generally in the teacher's classroom—it is important that the teacher move from behind her desk and talk to the parent as an equal. The teacher does not wish to adopt a teaching attitude to the parent, as she does to the children. A face-to-face relationship may be enhanced by both parties being seated comfortably in chairs. The purpose of the informal arrangement is to help the parent feel that she is a part of the same team to which the teacher belongs—that is, they are both working for the child's improvement.

To conduct a successful parent conference demands preparation and skill. Although the parent and the teacher ought to be working for the child's welfare, this purpose may become lost in the heat of battle if the conference is not well planned and executed. Langdon and Stout[13] have compiled the following list of some do's and dont's in conducting a parent interview:

1. Be truthful and honest.
2. Respect the parents' confidence.
3. Do not appear to be shocked by anything.
4. Don't jump to conclusions.
5. Take what parents say seriously.
6. Don't be authoritative.
7. Avoid getting into arguments.
8. Avoid teacherish, pedantic language.
9. Be sympathetically understanding but not sentimental.
10. Be ready to express honest admiration for what parents do.

---

[13] Grace Langdon and Irving W. Stout, *Teacher-Parent Interviews* (Englewood Cliffs, N.J.: Prentice-Hall, Inc., 1955), pp. 294–311.

11. Let parents have plenty of oportunity to talk about what concerns them.

12. Be ready and willing to explain.

13. Let it be seen that the parents are not expected to do all of the adjusting.

In addition to this excellent list of do's and dont's, the teacher must realize that she sets the tone for the interview and is largely responsible for its outcome. She must remain tactful and courteous and must avoid becoming defensive. Far too many teachers think that the purpose of a parent conference is to tell all the unfortunate and disturbing things that have happened to the parent's child during the school year. A conference is not the place for the teacher to unburden her problems at the parent's expense, but rather is a place to mend discordant feelings and to plan together for the benefit of the child. Many teachers fail to listen attentively enough to discover what is bothering the parents. Instead of listening, some teachers spend the time when the parent is talking in thinking of some answer to defend the school; consequently, the teacher in such an instance is in no position to discuss the problem at hand in an intelligent manner.

A well trained teacher soon overcomes the feeling of responsibility for reforming parents, and thus becomes less irritated at their lack of reform. When a teacher keeps her thoughts centered on helping the child, she pays less and less attention to her own personal feelings. Although parental criticism is hard to take, one can learn to look upon it as useful, both in revealing the parents' thinking and in pointing to things to which thought might well be given.[14] Parent conferences should end pleasantly with both the teacher and parent agreeing upon some plans for cooperation in helping the child. A record of each conference ought to be kept and filed away for future reference.

Greater Use of School Facilities

In an earlier chapter having to do with understanding and working with the community, the uses of school property, rules and regulations, and legal restrictions on the use of school plant were treated

---

[14] *Ibid.*, p. 195.

briefly. It is the purpose of this section of the book to emphasize that school facilities should be planned and maintained for expanded community use as well as for expanded school use. In many ways it is difficult to separate a strictly school use from a legitimate community use. The school facilities are, in many instances, used by either the children or the children's parents.

Earlier trends. If the school officials and the school board accept the concept of the school serving the community, then the many activities and devices inherent in such a belief will encourage a year round usage of school facilities. During early colonial times the school was used for purposes in addition to formal education. In New England the "little red school" was the center of community life; it was used for town meetings, socials, debates, and even religious services. The use of school buildings for community activities became greatly minimized as agrarian growth decreased and urban growth increased in the United States. This disuse of the schools by the community and the rise of certain socio-economic activities gave impetus to such organizations as the Y.M.C.A., Y.W.C.A., Boy Scouts, Girl Scouts, and women's clubs. From this trend grew a belief that school buildings should be used for "formal education" purposes only.

Modern trends. Today we have begun a return movement toward full-time use of school facilities. This changing trend is probably due to a great many factors and not to any one underlying principle. The trend of our populace in moving away from closely packed urban areas to suburban environments is a prime factor, as is the implication of "modern" education, which not only invites the adult population to make use of school buildings, but also permits children to use the school facilities in leisure time activities. The pecuniary interests of certain groups who believe it is a waste of money to let a major public tax investment, school buildings, be idle for three months a year has also had its effect on community use of school facilities.

Within the last two decades there has been a well defined movement toward making the school the center of community life. Thus, today the school buildings are being opened for the use of the general public during the evenings and at other times when the work of the regular pupils will not be hindered.

Besides being used by adult classes, the school plant is being used as a meeting place by innumerable associations, clubs, societies, and other organizations that are not prohibited from such use by legal barriers. Schools can play a much more realistic role than they have played in the past in making our communities become better integrated working units in our society. One of the first steps to be taken is the development of the community's physical facilities so that the real needs of the people are met.

Public school programs and building facilities are used by the youth of America and should not be isolated from the life of the community. The school must be conceived of as an institution whose program is based upon the needs of the people and to the community it serves.

Future planning. It is obvious that school facilities now available in most school communities are inadequate. If school buildings were not originally planned to serve extensively, rehabilitation may well be in order. People are living in a new age, with new aims, and with a philosophy which seeks to have each day contribute its maximum to human living and welfare.

While the existing school plant can be adapted to many community activities, its scope in the future could be broader. If the public continues to accept the school plants as areas for community use, then future construction should be planned to adequately house and facilitate these activities. The cost of such a project should be sufficiently supported in order to do justice to the activities.

Designing school plants for community use means that several factors must be given consideration. Among these are: location of facilities to be used by the community, distribution of heat, adequate storage space for equipment, special service features, and extra toilet facilities. Furthermore, after the plant is completed, extra custodial care as well as more frequent repairs will be needed. Extra supervision on the part of school personnel or employees of the school board will also be needed. Future plans should include advanced methods of scheduling community activities so they do not interfere with schoolwork and procedures for equitably deciding what groups may be permitted to use the school plant and under what conditions.

Community use of school facilities affords the school personnel a tremendous opportunity for good public relations. Persons who participate in a community program will tend to boost or to knock a school and its faculty according to their relations with educators and the cooperation given by them. Within the school program, faculty members can lend their support and efforts to worthwhile community projects.

The school plant is an indispensable agency for interpreting the activities and functions of the school to the people of the community. It serves to stimulate and to improve both group and individual contacts between school personnel and the public. More attention needs to be focused upon the school plant as an agent of interpretation if it is to make its maximum contribution to the total public relations program.

CHAPTER VII

Evaluating the Program

Appraisal as An Integral Part of Public Relations

The school administrator must have means for finding out in what ways the general program of public relations is proving to be satisfactory and in what ways it is proving unsatisfactory, and why. He needs to know how effectively each phase of the program is functioning and what changes, if any, are desirable. What parts of the program provoke public criticism? What portions of the program are working best? Answers to these and similar problems may be obtained through proper evaluation.

Evaluation is an integral part of the total public relations program. Every public relations program needs continuous examination and study in order for it to be kept in line with educational and social changes. The appraisal should be carefully planned under the direction of personnel who know what is to be done. Generally, the responsibility for evaluation rests with the board of education and superintendent of schools as the community's official representatives. Even though others are designated or employed for the purpose, the superintendent will almost inevitably occupy the central position in any program of evaluation and must accept responsibility for what is done. If he is wise, he will utilize the staff and the board of education, and will confer with laymen in order to obtain the data for evaluation purposes. It must be remembered that at all times the public is indirectly appraising the program in many ways.

Methods of Appraisal

As a program of public school relations proceeds there should be some evidence that it is accomplishing the objectives and purposes for which it was planned. This realization can come only through some effective appraisal of the results of the various activities included within the program. Appraisal in the area of public school relations is not easy. Most of the progress that has been made in the scientific evaluation of public relations concerns the use of score cards and related devices.

The number of program activities is not the criterion by which public relations should be judged. There is, unfortunately, no purely objective means of evaluating public relations programs and activities. However, until suitable methods are developed, appraisers will of necessity rely upon such means as informal methods, evaluation in terms of criteria or general principles, opinion polls and surveys, and check lists and rating scales.

Informal methods. Every administrator has some opportunity to informally evaluate the effects of various aspects or parts of the total public relations program. These informal evaluations may be incidental or they may be part of an organized plan. Perhaps the simplest form of evaluation is the observation of the relationships involved in public relations programs. The American Association of School Administrators[1] says in this regard:

> It requires no highly scientific instruments to gather pertinent information, for example, on the public relations contributions of teachers. If teachers are untrained or indifferent to the public relations effects of their own activities in or out of the classroom, the facts are easily determined. . . .
>
> Another informal means of evaluation is through the letters received by the school, written by parents and other citizens. . . .
>
> In the same category of incidental evaluation are the remarks of lay persons in the course of conversation. . . .
>
> Discussion groups in which laymen and school personnel participate are useful avenues for the evaluation of a public relations program.

These informal observations provide a storehouse of knowledge about certain aspects of the total program of public relations. One may add to the above list of observations the criterion of whether the community accepts or rejects the public relations program. Lay participation in discussions and debates of educational issues should be carefully analyzed through well directed questions. Such analysis should give some indication of the degree of educational understanding by citizens and of their concern for the improvement of the educational program.

---

[1] American Association of School Administrators, *Public Relations for America's Schools* (Washington, D.C.: The Association, 1950), pp. 261–62.

Although the evidence obtained by informal means of evaluation is highly subjective, it forms a picture from which an administrator can gain many suggestions for improving the public relations program.

Even though many appraisals must necessarily be subjective, it is desirable that they approach objectivity as much as possible. William A. Yeager[2] lists the following subjective methods as helpful: (1) informal questioning through conversation; (2) letters; (3) discussion groups; (4) press reports; (5) public interest and support; (6) pupil response; (7) requests for publications and services; and (8) group response. The director of the program may desire to take advantage of more objective procedures insofar as they are applicable to his program. Guesswork should be eliminated and opinion, wherever manifested, determined as reliably as possible.

Evaluation in terms of criteria or general principles. Through careful planning a superintendent and his staff may develop a comprehensive set of significant questions, based upon criteria or principles which may be used as a guide for appraising a public relations program. The questions developed may require a simple "yes" or "no" answer or may require the appraiser to estimate the degree of success. Questions that deal with the over-all program of public relations will have to be quite general in nature.

An investigation by William S. Vincent[3] presents those public school practices which tend to occur more frequently in better supported schools than in less well supported schools. For the basis of his study he used a guide prepared by Mort, Burke, and Fiske, entitled "A Guide for the Analysis and Description of Public School Services." Twelve objectives of education serve as the basis for the guide, with the eleventh objective pertaining to the maintenance of optimum relations between home and school and between community and school. Data from the study were secured from three sources: (1) reports based upon the guide filed by participating school systems; (2) check lists based upon the guide filed by field workers who visited schools; and (3) annual reports of school systems to the state department of education. Schools were rated on a

---

[2] William A. Yeager, *School-Community Relations* (New York: The Dryden Press, 1951), pp. 428–29.

[3] William S. Vincent, *Emerging Patterns of Public School Practice* (New York: Teachers College, Columbia University, 1945).

four-point (0–1–2–3) scale for each of the items covered in the guide. The study definitely showed that in all areas of school achievement the better supported schools did a notably better job than did the less well supported schools. This is particularly true in public relations.

Evaluation criteria can be used to measure the degree of success of the activities employed in the program, or they can be applied to the effects and outcomes of the program in terms of community response. Criteria of this type ought to help determine the changes in attitudes, opinions, appreciations, and understandings of school-community relations.

Opinion polls and surveys. Opinion polls can be used to determine the views of citizens on particular issues or problems in connection with the educational program. The need for changes in the public relations programs could be one of the problems for study.

In expressing general judgments of satisfaction or dissatisfaction, people often depend upon hunches, single experiences, hearsay, or personal likes and dislikes. Such judgments may be difficult to deal with, particularly if expressed by those with considerable influence; it must be recalled that it is natural for people to make judgments, however faulty their basis for so doing. The problem is to develop a more objective discriminating approach.

Frederick T. Rope[4] made a study in the Pittsburgh community relative to the assessment of community opinion in relation to certain issues involved in financing a public school system, and to the identification and appraisal of the influence of some factors which function in determining the structure of that opinion.

This study was made as a part of the survey of the Pittsburgh school system. An opinion questionnaire employing the interview technique was used to get responses. The cross section method of sampling was used in order to push beyond Pittsburgh's articulate organizations and pressure groups and to get the opinions which would be representative of all the people. The questionnaire was confined to financial issues because the extent of the educational offering of a community is determined in a large measure by the monetary support accorded the schools, and because centering the study upon clearcut issues of school support focused attention on

---

4 Frederick T. Rope, *Opinion Conflict and School Support* (New York: Teachers College, Columbia University, 1947).

the issues at hand. A significant conclusion reached by the study was that the people of Pittsburgh want and are willing to pay for broad educational services.

If proper sampling techniques are employed, opinion polls afford a cross sectional view of public opinion at any given time on any educational issue, practice, or proposal. By reflecting the attitudes of different groups on special issues or questions, they indicate where public relations efforts need to be altered or improved.

Public opinion on school issues can be ascertained by applying the scientific principles commonly employed in such public opinion surveys as the Gallup Polls. Paul A. Hedlund[5] developed an inexpensive method for measuring public opinion on school issues by applying these scientific principles. Through careful sampling of a relatively small representative group, it is possible by this method to determine the attitude of the total population. The reliability claimed for the method, when proper precautions are observed in sampling, is such that a sample of approximately 5 per cent of the total population indicates the opinion of the total population within 5 per cent of the true division of opinion.

In this study tenth-grade pupils were used to circulate written questionnaires. Each student submitted the names of two men and two women of his acquaintance, each representing a different household. Their instructions were to include two people over forty years of age and two under forty. Any foreign-born acquaintances and any person over sixty years old was to be included. The responses were analyzed to determine how well the sample corresponded to the total population with respect to sex, age, place of nativity, race, and economic status. The method was further validated by comparison with results obtained by sampling every thirty-eighth household listed in the city directory. Although scientific polling has not yet been widely used as a tool of the school administrator, according to Hedlund it has promise of becoming one.

In an opinion poll developed by Harold C. Hand,[6] he and his collaborators designed polling inventories for determining opinions of parents, teachers, upper elementary school pupils, and secondary

---

[5] Paul A. Hedlund, "Measuring Public Opinion of School Issues," *American School Board Journal,* CXVI (April, 1948), 29–30.

[6] Harold C. Hand, *What People Think About Their Schools* (New York: World Book Company, 1948).

school students about the schools, in terms of how well they are succeeding in their public relations practices, the specific points at which they are succeeding or failing, and consequent top priorities. Directions are given for the use of the inventories and the steps which must be taken to provide a proper analysis of the findings are indicated; suggestions are also made for reporting the findings and for practical use of the data obtained. Each inventory has been carefully pretested, revised, and actually used in one or more city-wide polls, with modifications as experience suggested. This is an excellent opinion poll and provides the basis for comparisons among different groups.

Check lists and rating scales. Numerous check lists and rating scales for evaluating public relations programs and activities have been developed, but most of them are unavailable for general use.

L. S. Michael[7] developed a five-point scale on twenty-nine selected public relations activities in an attempt to determine the most valuable school practices in promoting good public relations. Similarly, Charles S. Johnson[8] developed a rating scale and used it in the investigation of the public relations of six communities. The scale was based on research in the field of school public relations, on the experiences of school administrators, and on the opinions of interested people outside the profession. This scale was constructed to serve in an analytical appraisal of school-community relationships in the six selected villages investigated. This scale included twenty areas for survey—namely, administrative planning, costs, school surveys, annual reports, house organs, teacher's handbooks, non-teaching personnel, pupil publications, newspapers, exhibits and special events, report cards, parent-teacher associations, citizens' advisory councils, speakers' bureaus, service clubs, community welfare groups, youth organizations, church and school, local government, and the school plant.

One very thorough study in this area was made by Delmas Miller.[9] He developed an instrument based on the ratings of 234 selected

---

[7] L. S. Michael, "A Proposed Program of Improved Public Relations for the Schools of Wood County, West Virginia" (Unpublished doctoral dissertation, New York University, 1941).

[8] Charles S. Johnson, "A Comparative Study of School Public Relations" (Unpublished doctoral dissertation, New York University, 1943).

[9] Delmas F. Miller, "An Appraisal Technique for Programs of Public School Relations" (Unpublished doctoral dissertation, University of Pittsburgh, 1943).

jurors in the field of public relations. The jury represented the schools of each state which ranked highest (according to state superintendents) in public relations. Each juror was asked to rate as excellent, good, fair, or of no value those activities with which the jurors had had experience from among a list of 171 public school relations activities submitted by Miller. From these ratings, a score card was developed which, according to the author, may be used by the school administrator or his staff to appraise the public school relations activities of his own school system. When used in this self-appraising manner, Miller's score card affords an opportunity to evaluate the public school relations program in the light of comparative standards. In developing the Appraisal Form, Miller took into consideration the fact that philosophies regarding public school relations activities and programs may differ. Two separate sets of figures are therefore provided, one for such activities under a philosophy of *Educational Interpretation,* and the second based on the philosophy of *Child-Centered Mutual Cooperation.*

This study makes clear that a public relations program is determined by the needs of the school, and that the administration must assume responsibility for its operation. Further, it gives evidence that a score card can be helpful in appraising public relations.

L. W. Seyler[10] developed a tentative check list for school-home relationships to be used in the elementary field. After pertinent literature had been reviewed and many conferences with educators and parents had been held in order to select those items that seemed most suitable and objective, a preliminary check list was formulated. This consisted of eight large divisions. A qualified jury of sixty members was selected to judge the suitability of the check list. From their combined judgments the final check list of five main divisions, each with six subdivisions, was formulated. This revision was then sent out for use to 210 educators, who reported favorable results and expressed the desire for continued use of the check list in particular situations. All results were given as a summary and not as final norms.

As this check list was among the first to be developed for appraising public relations programs, considerable study and revision will be required in order to determine the validity and the reliability of

---

[10] L. W. Seyler, "A Tentative Check-List for School-Home Relationships" (Unpublished doctoral dissertation, University of California at Los Angeles, 1944).

the items used. It does represent an excellent step toward developing an appraisal instrument.

A check list for the evaluation of public school relations of public secondary schools was developed by F. W. Bainbridge.[11] His check list may be used to determine the status of public relations programs in secondary schools through a study of their underlying philosophies and the frequency with which certain policies and practices are employed. The latter are listed under such headings as: (1) information service; (2) curriculum; (3) extra-activities reaching into the community; (4) other school activities reaching into the community; (5) faculty contacts with the community; and (6) community use of buildings and equipment. A final part is designed to assist in evaluating the program as a whole and the results of a public relations program. Questions are asked as to the origin of the public relations program, its relation to the school's operating procedures, and the criteria used in judging its power to produce results. Provision is made for evaluation on a four-point scale in terms of improvements in such matters as pupil morale, teacher morale, and participation of patrons and citizens in school activities.

This check list is one of the better ones that has been developed. It provides for total evaluation and has undergone enough revision and refinement so that secondary school people will find this instrument very useful in appraising public relations.

Jacob F. Weins[12] attempted to make an objective evaluation of the present effectiveness of public school relations in the high schools of California. He reviewed the literature in the field of public school relations. Activities which might be objectively measured were listed on a preliminary appraisal form and sent to a jury of twenty experts in the field of public school administration and public relations, with directions to rate each activity. From the responses of fifteen jurors, a school public relations appraisal form was developed. Thirty California high schools, sampled according to size and geographic location, were selected for appraisal of their public relations programs. Each school was appraised by the principal and

---

11 F. W. Bainbridge II, "The Growth and Development of Public Relations in Public Secondary Schools of the United States" (Unpublished doctoral dissertation, Indiana University, 1950).

12 Jacob F. Weins, "An Evaluation of the Public School Relations in the High Schools of Small Cities and Rural Communities of California" (Unpublished doctoral dissertation, University of California at Los Angeles, 1950).

teachers of the school as well as by laymen of the community. Each
school was also appraised by the office of the county superintendent
of schools. A total of 162 appraisals were tabulated.

Other approaches.   Few standardized objective methods of appraising public relations programs have been developed. Many programs of public relations are not highly enough developed to encourage administrators to evaluate them or to compare them in some
formal way with those of other districts. Yet there are many ways
which administrators may find useful and helpful if they really seek
to discover how well they are doing in this regard. One such study
gives the following criteria for the evaluation of public relations
within a district:[13] (1) opinions of professional employees; (2)
opinions of non-teaching employees; (3) opinions of individuals and
groups in the community; (4) simple observations by administrators; (5) remarks of lay persons in ordinary conversation; (6) discussion groups; (7) letters; (8) public interest and support; (9)
pupil response; and (10) requests for school publications and
services. It is always appropriate to utilize community citizens in
the appraisal function; this is especially true if they have been active
in program development.

An administrator who wishes to evaluate the public relations
program may need to use more than one method of appraisal. Any
of the methods of appraisal presented in this chapter may be used for
a particular school or school system, as it will be helpful in analyzing the community backgrounds and problems which are condition-
ing factors in the educational program and public relations. It may
be necessary to diagnose community attitudes in order to evaluate
public relations practices in terms of their suitability for dealing with
the groups and individuals comprising the community.

The Effects of Public Relations Activities

Difficult to determine.   The professional literature in education
contains numerous status studies of public relations programs and
activities, but few observed tests of their effects have been noted.
The activities found in effective public relations programs are ex-
tremely difficult to isolate and study because establishing controlled

---

[13] Dale Baughman, "Yardsticks for Measuring School-Community Relations,"
Educational Administration and Supervision, XLIII (January, 1957), 19.

situations for evaluation is not easy. Likewise, the interrelationship of these activities under differing environments causes much concern when one attempts to decide the total effects of any selected activity. Deciding the kind of effects to investigate represents one of the most formidable problems in school public relations research. This is true partly because so little guidance is available in the professional literature and partly because of the complexity of the "effect" problem in studying any type of mass communication media. The fact that several media may be used to promote one phase of school activities adds to the arduous task of determining the "effect" of any given medium.

More research needed.   There is ample evidence to indicate that research in school public relations has endured the lack of an analytical model of the public relations process with which to arrange research problems in the order of their significance. In addition to this glaring need, much research is needed in the further development and refinement of measures for evaluating the various public relations activities and practices and for determining the conditions under which they may function most effectively.

Further investigations of the potentialities of the school board as an agency for the promotion of public relations programs should prove rewarding. There is an apparent need for research on methods and techniques for the in-service education of school board members in order that they may function more efficiently in the public relations program. Research is needed to identify the specific practices and other considerations associated with parent satisfaction and dissatisfaction with the public schools. More investigations should be made of the potential for public relations held by pupils, teachers, and non-teaching personnel in the public relations program. It appears that a fruitful area for further study would be concerned with determining what teachers know about their schools and the school districts in which they work. Finally, more research is needed to determine the type of training that is most effective in preparing teachers and other school personnel for public relations service.

CHAPTER VIII

Summary

A significant function of public relations is to develop an awareness of the importance of education in your community. Public relations embodies all the relationships that exist in a two-way exchange of ideas between the school and the community, and provides the basis for mutual understanding. Almost every phase of school work has some effect upon the relationship between the schools and the community.

The Nature and Purpose of Public Relations

Although there has been an increase in both the amount of research and the number of people doing research in public relations since the middle 1920s, many problems remain unresolved. The need for better public relations programs may be seen by studying the possibilities for improvement, the changing school patterns, citizen information, changing faculty status, public opinion of teachers, and pressure groups.

School public relations began with the creation of the State Board of Education in Massachusetts when Horace Mann first explained to the American people the meaning and importance of public education. Formal recognition of public relations came much later. This recognition was accompanied by an increased interest in our schools on the part of the public. Furthermore, there has been an upsurge of lay participation in educational planning. Public relations plays a significant role in the education of our youth, as the students of today will be the parents and citizens of tomorrow and will have a voice in how our future schools are operated.

The general purpose of public relations in schools is to keep the public informed regarding the purposes, accomplishments, conditions, and needs of the schools. There are many publics to be understood and to be satisfied, not just one general audience. Therefore, the school must keep the child's welfare, as well as the important needs of society, as its central focus.

Understanding and Working with the Community

In order to develop and maintain an effective program of public relations it is necessary to comprehend the community. Many helpful data may be secured from the United States Census reports. The administrator needs information about the community that is representative of the total community. In a like manner, the community needs information about the schools. Survey reports give the school officials and the general public impartial data about the nature of the community, its people, its resources, its institutions, and some of its problems.

Studies of public opinion provide the school district with information about how the people in the community feel regarding school issues and about what they desire from the schools. In working with the community it is essential that the administrator have some guides to action. The principles of public relations provide some of this assistance, and also serve as helpful aids to the development of an effective program.

Parents have a desire for knowledge about the school, but they do not always make the necessary effort to obtain it. Perhaps the crux of the matter lies in the fact that the manner in which the publics think of education is determined to some extent by what they know about it.

To understand community life, one must comprehend the structure of the community. This includes all the important functions by which a local population maintains itself; as well as their interrelations.

There has been a trend in recent years toward greater community use of school facilities. The school may well capitalize on this trend by the promotion of cordial relationships with community agencies. Boards of education generally have wide discretionary powers to regulate the use of school facilities, and they are particularly concerned that the property not be used for purposes contrary to the aims of education.

Community resources comprise the total educative objects, materials, and experience to be found in the area surrounding a school. Resources of the community are represented by institutions, services, materials, and processes. Some commonly used procedures for the utilization of community resources include contests, lectures, interviews, school trips, surveys, and work experiences.

Organization and Administration

The nature of the public relations program needs to be determined by a carefully considered philosophy, and should contain definitive goals, objectives, and patterns of organization. Prevailing types of organization include those directed by the superintendent of schools, by an administrative staff officer, by a director of public relations, by principals of the various schools, or by teacher committees.

The school board occupies a strategic position in public relations through its work as a board and the position of its members as individuals in the community. The school board as a body may serve as a means of liaison between the school and the public. As individuals, the school board may defend, support, and interpret the schools, at the same time as it investigates complaints and charges against them.

The school's chief executive officer is the person charged with responsibility for the public relations program. His task is to organize the machinery for school-community relationships toward unified operation. The superintendent is responsible to the board of education for all phases of the conduct of the schools.

Other factors that influence the organization of public relations programs include the internal structure of the local unit, the size of the school district in terms of pupil population, the amount of money available for school purposes, and the efficiency of the personnel employed.

The Staff and Public Relations

Every member of the school staff has a responsibility in public relations and should be made familiar with the general objectives of the program, as well as with the special techniques and procedures applicable at his particular level. Every act of the school staff has some effect on public relations. The director of the public relations program plays an important role in the leadership given to the program. The principal is a key figure in the individual school through his contacts with parents and citizens and through his professional and interpersonal relationships with his staff. The teacher comes closer to the home than any other worker in the school, and may be the first to sense public approval or disapproval. The pupils themselves constitute an important phase of public relations. The character, conduct, and achievements of the pupils daily reflect the influence of the school, and the pupils interpret the school to their parents. Non-instructional employees of the school must be included in the public relations programs; it is important that their position within the school be understood by the public and that they be good interpreters to the public in their own right.

Media of Public Relations

Wise judgment must be exercised in selecting various agencies, avenues, and media for public school relations. The entire school program should be interpreted to the public, and citizens should be informed of new practices and innovations in education, together with the reasons for their adoption. Some phases of the school program have received attention in public relations programs, almost to the exclusion of others. Among media most often used are pupils, parents and parent organizations, community groups, school reports and publications, personal contacts, special events, newspapers, radio, and television. Successful teaching helps to develop mutual understanding between the school and community and rates high in terms of effective media.

The School Plant

The purposes of the school plant are to facilitate instruction and to house the children and the school program. Procedures for planning school facilities are closely related to the competencies of the professional staff and their willingness to make long range plans. Lay persons ought to be involved in planning school facilities whenever possible. The dedication ceremony at a new plant offers an excellent opportunity for the promotion of public relations, as it gets parents and citizens into the school buildings.

The trend toward more creativity in the design of school plants and the idea of thinking of a school building as something other than an aggregation of classrooms are both forward looking concepts that emphasize the importance of the school plant in public relations. These trends also make for more functional buildings.

Operating, maintaining, and beautifying the school plant along with its site and grounds adds a touch of beauty and serves to preserve property values and develop good will. School visitors tend to think of the school program in the same way as they think of the plant and the personnel who operate and maintain it.

The use of the telephone, correspondence, and parent conferences usually takes place within the school plant. Each of these activities may be considered a device for developing public understanding and good will toward the school, if properly used.

The increase in use of school plants will, of necessity, be accompanied by planning which considers the special facilities needed for community use of the plant and facilities.

Evaluating the Program

Responsibility for evaluation of a school public relations program rests with the board of education and the superintendent of schools, with the latter occupying the central position. The various activities within the program should be appraised in the light of the objectives and purposes for which they were planned. Appraisal methods include informal methods, evaluation in terms of criteria or general principles, opinion polls and surveys, check lists and rating scales. Informal methods are necessarily subjective, as they are based on observation of the school system and lay participation in discussions and debates on educational issues. Evaluation in terms of criteria and principles may be somewhat more objective, calling for responses to a set of pertinent questions. Opinion polls and surveys, when properly employed, afford a cross sectional view of public opinion at any time on any educational issue, practice, or proposal. Several check lists and rating scales for evaluating public relations programs and activities have been developed, but unfortunately only a few are available for general use.

Bibliography

Bailey, Stephen K., *et al.*, *Schoolmen and Politics*. Syracuse: Syracuse University Press, 1962.

Bast, Margaret, and Jeannette Riddle, "Improvement of Community Relations Provides Understanding Needed to Gain School Support," *Ohio Schools*, XLII (March, 1964), 25.

Baughman, M. Dale, "The School's Role In Community Life," *School and Community*, LI (October, 1964), 9–10.

Carter, Richard V., "Voters and Their Schools," *The Phi Delta Kappan*, XLIX (February, 1961), 244–249.

Dapper, Gloria, *Public Relations for Educators*. New York: The Macmillan Company, 1964.

Dunfee, Maxine, "What Do Parents Need to Know?", *Educational Leadership*, XXII (December, 1964), 162–163.

Finchum, R. N., "Let's Make The Most of Our School Custodians," *School Life*, XLVII (December, 1964), 29–31.

Fischer, John H., and Muriel Crosby, "Community and Its Schools," *Children*, XI (January, 1964), 3–12.

Folk, Chris, "Interpreting the Secondary School," *The High School Journal*, XLVIII (January, 1965), 257–261.

Gambold, Willard, J., "Developing Good Community Relations," *Education*, LXXXIV (November, 1963), 131–136.

House, F. Wayne, "Discovering and Utilizing Community Resources," *The National Business Education Quarterly*, XXXI (May, 1963), 58–62.

Jones, C. V., "Developing Community Understanding For Educational Innovation," *The American School Board Journal*, CXLIX (July, 1964), 29.

Jones, James J., and Irving W. Stout, *School Public Relations: Issues and Cases*. New York: G. P. Putnam's Sons, 1960.

Kindred, Leslie W., ed., *Communications Research and School-Community Relations*. Philadelphia: Cooperative Research Program of the Office of Education, and College of Education, Temple University, 1965.

Kindred, Leslie W., "Assistant Superintendent—Community Relations," *Preparation Programs for School Administrators*. East Lansing, Michigan: Michigan State University, 1963.

Kindred, Leslie W., *School Public Relations*. Englewood Cliffs, N.J.: Prentice-Hall, Inc., 1957.

Langdon, Grace, and Irving W. Stout, *Helping Parents Understand Their Child's School*. Englewood Cliffs, N.J.: Prentice-Hall, Inc., 1957.

Lewis, Anne E., "Better Press Relations For Schools," *Theory Into Practice*, (October, 1964), 149–153.

McCloskey, Gordon, *Education and Public Understanding.* New York: Harper and Row, Publishers, 1959.

Miller, James L., "Community Resources," *Grade Teacher,* LXXXII (February, 1965), 118–121.

Moehlman, Arthur B., and James A. van Zwoll, *School Public Relations.* New York: Appleton-Century-Crofts, Inc., 1957.

Pullen, Milton V., "Classroom Guidance: Interpreting the School Program to Parents," *The Instructor,* LXXIV (February, 1965), 24–25.

Rinker, L. G., "School Board and the Newspaper," *The American School Board Journal,* CLXIX (October, 1964), 22.

Schwirian, Kent P., "Testing at Issue: A Case Study of School and Community Conflict," *Theory into Practice,* II (October, 1963), 226–234.

Stearns, Harry L., *Community Relations and the Public Schools.* Englewood Cliffs, N.J.: Prentice-Hall, Inc., 1955.

Stout, Irving W., and Grace Langdon, "What Parents Want to Know About Their Child's School," *Nation's Schools,* LX (August, 1957), 45–48.

Sumption, Merle R., *How to Conduct A Citizens School Survey,* Englewood Cliffs, N.J.: Prentice-Hall, Inc., 1952, Chapter 10.

Tirado, Ramon Claudia, "A Different Approach to School and Community Relations in a Depressed Community," *The Journal of Educational Sociology,* XXXVI (March, 1963), 310–318.

Tope, Donald D., *et al., The Social Sciences View School Administration.* Englewood Cliffs, N.J.: Prentice-Hall, Inc., 1965.

Watson, Eugene R., "Utilization of School Facilities for Adult Education during the Summer," *The High School Journal,* XLVII (March, 1964), 253–259.

Williams, Frederick, and Barbara Sundene, "A Field Study in Effects of a Public Relations Speech," *The Journal of Communication,* XV (September, 1965), 161–170.

Wilson, Charles H., "On These Issues Superintendents Stand or Fall," *Nation's Schools,* LXXV (June, 1965), 27–29.

Wilson, Roy K., "Are Madison Avenue Public Relations Techniques Good Enough for the Schools?" *Bulletin of the National Association of Secondary School Principals,* XLVIII (April, 1964), 79.

Yeager, William A., *School-Community Relations.* New York: The Dryden Press, 1951.

Index

Index